My Rich Prince

My Rich Prince

Notes For My Son

Dr Okechukwu Michael Mwim

Matador
9 Priory Business Park,
Wistow Road, Kibworth Beauchamp,
Leicestershire. LE8 0RX
Tel: 0116 279 2299
Email: books@troubador.co.uk
Web: www.troubador.co.uk/matador
Twitter: @matadorbooks

ISBN 978 1788037 525

British Library Cataloguing in Publication Data.
A catalogue record for this book is available from the British Library.

Printed on FSC accredited paper
Printed and bound in Great Britain by 4edge Limited
Typeset in 11pt Adobe Garamond Pro by Troubador Publishing Ltd, Leicester, UK

To Courage, Persistence and Determination

Contents

1 There are two types of people 1
1.1 The builder and the architect 1
1.2 Cameos and stuntmen 4
1.3 First an idea 5
1.4 Dispensable 6
1.5 Man's best friend 8
1.6 A tale of two people 9
1.7 Cause and effect 10
1.8 Take God out of the equation 12
1.9 Waiting for the saviour 14

2 They don't have to like you 15
2.1 At the beginning 15
2.2 Be yourself 16
2.3 Start with loving yourself 17
2.4 Life as a party 18
2.5 Life is too long for a selfish person 20
2.6 Remain different 21
2.7 On appearance and race 23

3 Learn early to say no 26
3.1 Again, love yourself 26
3.2 Then you have to believe, in yourself 27

3.3 So what is no? (Like cat and dog)   29
3.4 Say no   31
3.5 Other forms of no   34
3.6 It depends on you   34
3.7 It is <u>always</u> down to you   35
3.8 Dr P   37
3.9 Pick your fights   38
3.10 Take home   39

4   **Heaven can wait**   **40**
4.1 We're talking about life here on Earth   40
4.2 Talking of Heaven, whose heaven?   41
4.3 To get to heaven, you would have to die first   44
4.4 Start with the end in mind   46
4.5 Sheep move as a herd   48
4.6 Reward yourself though for successes   50
4.7 Before you buy   51
4.8 You need more than trust   53
4.9 Smokescreens   55
4.10 You have no right   56
4.11 Don't get rich quick   57
4.12 There are lots of things to worry about,
     girls are not one of them   59
4.13 Pray   61

5   **Love**   **63**
5.1 Candles   63
5.2 Show love   65
5.3 You never know   66
5.4 Which love? What love?   67
5.5 Stupid love   68
5.6 Love hurts   71
5.7 Feel love   72

6 Don't forget money   73

6.1 The origin   73
6.2 Forms of money   74
6.3 The ways people see money   75
6.4 How do you see money?   76
6.5 0 (Zero) and X people   76
6.6 Don't ignore money   77
6.7 Is money bad?   79
6.8 You decide   81
6.9 But beware   82
6.10 Easy money   83
6.11 Borrowed money card   85
6.12 Learn to handle money   86
6.13 The buck stops with you   88

7 The butterfly effect   89

7.1 Catch 'em young   89
7.2 Argunga Fishing Festival   90
7.3 Focus   92
7.4 The power of compounding   95
7.5 What doesn't kill you   95

8 Live!   99

8.1 The worrier   99
8.2 Problems keep floating   101
8.3 Don't bang your head   103
8.4 Don't confuse persistence with stubbornness   104
8.5 Knowledge is not power   105
8.6 Switch off the TV   106
8.7 What if you die tonight?   107
8.8 Live with passion   109

Preamble

Being rich should never be seen just in monetary terms, as it instead does extend to several things and implies much more than how much money one has stacked up in a bank account.

Of most importance, in my opinion, is the richness of character that is more reliably achieved when the various facets of one's life work together like the different parts of a well-oiled engine. This is likely to lead to a life that flows in the direction of the ocean of self-fulfilment, one of the ultimate of goals. My hope is that the words contained in this book act as constant guide and reminder on the intermittently tortuous path you are very likely to follow. Good luck, my son.

1

There are two types of people

1.1   The builder and the architect

History books are full of men and women who were able to achieve great and mighty feats in their lives. We are often told of how such people were able to overcome all sorts of obstacles in order to achieve their goals.

What is common for the people who have made a name for themselves in the past is the possession of clear ideas and having strong beliefs they will achieve their goals. At times, this was also mixed with vision and their ability to see things most other people could not see.

The subsequent status of these achievers in society is clear and is never questioned. They in fact receive so much acknowledgement that the men and women who actually did the (often physical) work, behind the scenes, get forgotten. The ones in the battlefield, if we're talking about wars; the ones who did the actual construction of the wonderful bridges and houses, if we're talking about architectural designs, never get mentioned.

For a house to get built for instance, an architect would have to draw a plan of what the house should be like – how many rooms would be in the house, how the rooms would be connected to each other; the general and structural design of the house.

Assuming the house to be built is a government one, the architect then hands over the drawings on completion to the government officials. The government officials in turn then get a contractor, who hires the builders. While the contractor oversees things on a day-to-day basis, it is the builders who do all the work.

Architect
↓
draws a plan and hands over to
↓
potential House Owner/Government official
↓
who
↓
gets a Building Contractor
↓
Building Contractor hires
↓
Workmen

The architect is ultimately responsible for the functionality and the stability of the house when finished. Which other professional, say a structural engineer, the architect works together with to achieve this is more or less his decision. If the house ultimately turns out to be impractical it is seen as the architect's fault.

There is, for instance, the unconfirmed story in Vienna about an architect who committed suicide after the house he designed was built. He got the contract to design a very important house for the city of Vienna. All went well and the house turned out to be very beautiful after it was built. It was a sure way of making a name for the architect and the house was guaranteed to ensure that his name found its way into the history books – which was what happened. He became very well known, except that it was for the wrong reasons. He committed a fatal error – he forgot to add toilets in the design of this very large and beautiful government house. The people did not forgive him for this mistake, and he became the laughing stock of the country and a source of shame for his colleagues and profession.

I have, however, never heard anybody apportion any form of blame on the contractor, or on his builders who in fact did the actual building. They do not get mentioned at all. They were only working for the wages, and this was what they got. The architect was, however, responsible for the whole project, and is accordingly rewarded or discredited, as the case may be. If things go grossly contrary to plans it will cost him dearly – might cost him everything. This is something he has to live with.

If things go, on the other hand, accordingly, he would become a hero and would be invited to dine with kings and queens and with presidents of countries.

The same kind of thing happened with the very popular *Titanic*, probably the most iconic ship in history. The tragic story of the then largest ship afloat is well known. It was the person who designed it that took all the blame when the *Titanic* sank and took the blame for the ship not being the huge and pioneering success he expected it to be. While the exact circumstance of his death remains blurred, what is clear is that he sank with the *Titanic* on 14 April 1912 during her maiden voyage, after hitting an iceberg. It is also unclear if he would have been able to save himself or if it suited him better to experience the same tragic end as the most popular ship in history. It is not difficult to imagine what kind of recognition and honour a safe trip with the *Titanic* would have brought him.

I have, on the other hand, never read, seen or heard anything about the men who did the real construction of the *Titanic*. What kind of people were they? How did they live their lives? Were they really just men, or did they have women builders as well? What was it like for them building the *Titanic*? Did any of them lose their lives during the construction? The answer to all the questions is the same – who cares! They were employed to do their work; they got paid at the end of the day – end of story. There is no possibility of subsequent reward, recognition or legacy. Such salient incentives are usually only reserved for a select few, those higher up the pyramid.

1.2   Cameos and stuntmen

A stuntman typically performs very challenging and dangerous scenes in films and television and then is 'edited out' of the scenes that audiences later see. They are replaced with images of the main characters, including that of the person who could then be portrayed as the 'hero'. So, the person you see involved in the dangerous car crash scene, fall from a great height or blown into the air (and still survives) is normally not the 'real' character but a stuntman, whose job it is to play such a role, for a fee. The only acknowledgement they could receive is that of their names being listed in the roll call of performers at the end of the film. The list is, however, usually so long and names written in such small print that they are barely legible; that is if the audience has not already left the cinema or switched off the film.

It is normal practice usually for contracts signed by stuntmen to include clauses that would mean that instances of injury (or even death) during their performance would still be used. In other words, if one were to die in the process of performing as a stuntman, the person would often have agreed that the accident will still be used in the real film. Take a moment to think about this and at the same time reflect, in contrast, on what is likely to happen if the main character in the film were to get injured (or, horror of horror, killed) during filming.

Think also of the fact that the Oscars, as far as I know, during its nearly ninety-year history does still not see the need to recognise the people who carry out such dangerous jobs in any shape or form. There is no category for them. They are not mentioned and, therefore, officially do not exist. It would look as if men and women who engage in these very important but dangerous roles are, on the other hand, quite dispensable.

1.3   First an idea

You know it all starts with an idea. Somebody has certainly got to, first of all, come up with the ideas; just as somebody has equally got to do the execution of the plan. These ideas or plans do still need to be implemented for it to be called a reality.

I have, if I come to think of it, never come across the names of people who merely executed other people's plans in history books. They don't get mentioned. They could have done a wonderful job, but nonetheless are not worthy of getting mentioned.

One of the reasons they get ignored could be because somebody had already gone through the trouble of drawing the map, or coming up with the idea they were to execute. All they had to do was just do as the plan said. In the scenario with the architect, until he finished and presented the plan for the building, the people around could neither see nor actually imagine such a house being built there, not to mention the design. So, coming up with the idea and outlining a way of making it work is the difficult part.

One could also argue that the builders, like the soldiers in the forefront of a battle, are exposed to fewer risks, and hence get less praise, unlike their more senior commanding officers, but I do not think so. The exposure to risk is certainly as high, if not higher, than that of the person leading them. The leader, whose idea is being executed, could have a sense of responsibility for all the members of the group which one can argue makes the burden on him more, but the personal risks could be the same or even more for the executors of the plan. It is only when one takes what the person who came up with the idea stands to gain if all goes according to plan into consideration that one would want to tend to believe that the level of exposure to risk is more, if the idea does not work out, that is. If things, however, go according to plans, and the wonderful idea on paper also becomes a brilliant idea in reality, the person who came up with the idea stands to make astronomical gains. This level of return on the time and the energy spent then means that the amount of return is commensurate with the risk.

This is certainly not the case at the private level. For if you come to think about it, the worst thing that would happen to the workmen if the project fails, for whatever reason, is that they would lose their source of income, which is temporal anyway. All they would then need do is to go looking for the next job. In the example with the Viennese architect, the building contractor and his workmen would have been paid their full wages. They did what they were supposed to do. The person who really suffers greatly, and who could lose everything if something of significance goes wrong, and who is therefore exposed to the most risk, is the person with the most responsibility – in this case the architect. It makes sense that they are the ones who get mentioned and not the rest.

Yet another example could be given with the surgeon carrying out a very complicated and less-routinely done surgical procedure. This surgeon normally works with the assistance of other medical professionals – junior doctors, anaesthetists, and possibly other doctors whose professional opinions were sought prior to the surgery. He or she also makes use of the support of nurses and other paramedics, without whose help it would be impossible to carry out surgery. I will leave you to imagine who gets mentioned and recognised no matter the outcome of the new and innovative surgery.

1.4   Dispensable

I think that the major difference, and the reason why only one person gets mentioned, and not as much breath gets wasted on the rest is due to the simple fact that the rest of the team could be said to be very dispensable. It wouldn't take much to get men and women with such skills, or even to teach people to whom such skills are new. So, while they play very important roles in the accomplishment of the said goal, what they do is not really unique if one comes to think about it. So, it finally makes sense, for who would you acknowledge more – the person without whom the project would remain a fantasy or the person whose position could quite easily have been replaced by somebody else?

So it is everywhere you find yourself. It will be a lot of hard work and it will often mean either working harder than the rest or going in a different direction than the others. The aim should be to make yourself as indispensable as possible wherever you find yourself. Make yourself as needed as absolutely possible. One of the early lessons one learns in house renovation is which walls and pillars in buildings not to mess with, and which, if you do, puts the house at risk of coming crashing down. Make yourself that pillar, as much as possible.

I was once with a well-travelled uncle of yours, who is well known to you. We were in an important building in the UK. This building had pictures of very important men, who though long dead, had major roles to play in the history of the UK. This uncle of yours drew our attention to those pictures and basically said, "You see these men, they are long dead but their pictures are still on display here because they did great things and are therefore still respected. The challenge we face is to go back to where we come from, where we are needed, and be useful enough, to the point that our pictures will someday also adorn the walls of some public building in years to come. We can otherwise continue to forever live in the shadows of their greatness in a society where we would not be able to do much more than just exist. The choice to branch out and walk on the less trodden path, with its risk and potential reward, or continue on the present path, towards a life of mediocrity is entirely ours". I found that view quite interesting, but guess that the difference for you is that, unlike me, your own reality is that you have less need to 'go back to where we come from' in order to make a remarkable difference. The world has also become much smaller, so much so that even the slightest 'noise' at one end of the world is these days sometimes even heard first at the other end.

1.5   Man's best friend

In a farm, the animals have their levels of usefulness. One of the most hardworking and useful is the dog. The dog makes the life of the farmer easier. It helps the farmer in many of the farming activities, especially where other animals are involved. The dog is, for instance, of much use during hunting activities. It also helps to round up the sheep when they have finished grazing and need to be brought back to the farmhouse. The dog also generally helps guard over the farm, especially against intruders and thieves.

Both the sheep and the pig, for instance, can hardly take care of themselves, let alone taking care of somebody else or assisting the farmer. Forget the lovely story that was portrayed in the film *Babe* ,in which the pig raised by sheepdogs learned to herd sheep and took part in the sheepherding context. Such incidents are unfortunately limited to the scenes of a movie. This class of animals normally loves its food and would rather hang around waiting to either be fed or to be shown where to get feed. They do not have to do much. The sheep and the pig could see themselves as being very smart since they have such wonderful lives, but yet do not have to do anything to sustain their lifestyle. They could, in that case, most certainly see the dog as very stupid. It does all the work and follows the farmer around, apparently being motivated by being thrown pieces of bones and left-over food once in a while.

Problem is that they cannot see beyond their short noses. They also are not able to see the bigger picture. They walk around in a state of somnambulism but are convinced they are awake. They would otherwise have realised certain painful truths, say that the farmer never kills the dog for food. Never. The farmer actually cries when his friend the dog dies and disposes of it properly. The pig and the sheep are, however, the first to be sold or killed for meat. They fail to realise that the only reason they are well fed is so that they will grow fat and therefore be either sold for good money or to produce good meat when they get slaughtered.

All the animals have, of their own accord, shaped their own destinies. The consequences of their decisions will follow them all the days of their lives, and even for generations to come. Sad bit is that they will still blame others, the farmer who kills or sells them for money inclusive, for their fates.

1.6   A tale of two people

It was said, by Tuco, in the old film classic, *The Good, the Bad and the Ugly*, that "there are two kinds of people in the world, my friend. Those who have a rope around their neck and those who have the job of doing the cutting". Another dimension to this quote is that there are those who tend to have a rope round their necks and then those who would enjoy making a show of doing the cutting. My reason for this addition will become obvious later, but I would now like to add that the person who has the rope around his neck has the rope around his neck as long as he has the rope around his neck, and this is obvious to the person supposed, or expected, to cut the rope. Looks as if I have taken a simple sentence and made it complicated. Well, not really. Here is what I mean. The person who has the knife and is to cut the other person free knows that, until the other person no longer has the rope around his neck, he has to dramatise the process of sharpening his knife and to enjoy his position as a saviour. As long as he has not performed the final act of actually cutting the rope – which in itself would take less than a second – he can freely parade himself as the next Jesus. The problem is that he knows this.

A man called Tolstoy wrote about something similar a long time ago. He preferred to see the two people described above as the oppressor and the oppressed. He thought they had a funny, yet dependent existence; that the oppressor loves the oppressed. So much so that he in fact will do everything for him. That he will sympathise with the oppressed, nurse his wounds and tend them. That he will do everything for the oppressed to show his love. But there is only one thing the oppressor will never do: he won't get off the back of the oppressed.

There is no oppressor without the oppressed, for the oppressor (or the oppressed) cannot live in isolation. You cannot have one without the other. The absence or non-existence of one makes the relevance of the other completely superfluous.

Which type of the two you would rather be is entirely up to you. That is the amazing thing about life. You're free to choose.

I know you will be wondering how somebody can decide to always have a rope round his or her neck, especially when they have the opportunity to decide otherwise.

I can only promise you that the whole subject is not very easy to explain. It is like trying to explain to you that you should have a shower before going to bed after an intensive game of football. It took a bit of time to sink in. Taking a shower for you had a direct link to dressing up and going out, not going to bed. Well, thank goodness you have realised that you definitely sleep better after those showers.

So, you now at least know why you have a restless night after such days full of activities if you do not have a shower.

This on its own is already a point for you.

1.7   Cause and effect

The problem with the people who always have a rope round their necks is that they are fully aware of the fact that something is wrong, but they somehow are not able to figure out what it is, nor are they able to work out what could be done about things.

They are much behind you in this manner of thinking since you are at least in the process of learning the law of cause and effect.

Identifying the problem is the first and most important step.

The easiest thing for such people is to make themselves believe that they mainly have bad luck in life. They think that if they didn't have such bad luck, how else could it be that they always have to rely on others to bail them out? Hence, they continue doing what they always did, which is not much more than waiting for the next saviour.

The problem is not with having bad luck once in a while. It is bound to happen. Bad luck is one of such things we cannot completely run away from.

The worst thing is when such bad luck becomes very repetitive. It is then more than just bad luck. There is an Igbo proverb that says that 'after an old woman has had her third fall, she is bound to count the contents of her basket'. Such occurrences are then less likely to be attributed purely to coincidence.

The problem is that most people, after going through the same misfortune several times, would be expected to pause a little and reflect on things. No, what they do is find excuses to make them believe that they are just victims. Victims of circumstances they cannot change. They accept defeat, and then blame others and external forces. You then hear such sentences like, "If only…"

They then start to blame others for their circumstances. They are not to blame. Of course, they are victims of circumstances they believe to be out of their reach.

At this point the noose has started to tighten.

Then appears the saviour who offers to cut them free.

Only problem is that he would do it at his convenience and based on his terms and conditions. Why should he do otherwise?

Worst problem is that the man with the rope around his neck thinks that the person doing the cutting is doing it because he is such a nice person who loves saving souls. Because he himself is good at heart and possibly somewhat naive, he expects everybody to be the same way.

I want to tell you something, my son – as an adult people expect you to be able to take care of yourself. That is the fundamental bottom line. It is seen as part of what makes one a human being. You have yourself to blame if you do not succeed in your endeavours, and I would have failed in my duty as your father if I am not able to make you realise this very important point. The ability to take care of yourself is one of the features you have as a human being. Be ready to have yourself to blame if you are not able to look after yourself. See this as your responsibility. It is not a shared responsibility, but exclusively yours and yours alone. You take over this responsibility when you cease to be a child. An adult who is unable to do this, except for when they lack the capability, say due to cognitive deficiencies, should not feel insulted by being treated as a child, who needs to be taken care of.

1.8   Take God out of the equation

So, what does God do? you may ask. What is his role in this?

What he does in this case is easy. He loves everybody equally.

Those who are good at cutting ropes, because they practise it so often that they are perfect in it, God makes even better in the art of rope cutting. This way they can cut even more ropes.

And those who are good at having ropes cut down from their neck? Well, I can only imagine that God will make their necks even better for carrying ropes.

I want you to think about those who expect God to come down and save them from the rope around their necks. I think he will feel both disappointed and let down by such people. He must wonder, "If I am going to be coming all the time to cut the rope around this young man's neck why did I then bother to waste my time making him in my image?" I think he will feel really let down.

I tell you, my son, that one of the worst things a man can do is to not take his own fate in his hands. Even God will not be happy with that, for why then did he create man in his own image and give him unlimited powers? Why did he make you both special and unique? Man's dominance of the world is so obvious that it is one of the areas where there is general agreement both in those who believe in the existence of God and those who do not.

So, there are two types of people in the world, those who have ropes, which they cannot cut, round their necks and those who do the cutting. You similarly have those people that, you will learn, are usually referred to as the masses, just as you have those few that were able to somehow climb above the rest, so that when the talk is about the masses, it is clear that they are not being referred to, for they have been able to rise above the generally easily dispensable mediocrity that the masses in reality are aligned to.

1.9   Waiting for the saviour

There are several people who have come to see and accept themselves as the downtrodden; the victims of society. There are even lots of instances where such beliefs, for whatever reason, have been handed down from one generation to the next. This belief and attitude of helplessness gets accepted by the people involved with time. For many people, this is when the real problem starts, for they then give up long before the journey has even started. They accept defeat without putting up any form of fight. To them their stance makes sense – which is, why bother when it would certainly not make any difference, why start at all, why waste the time and energy?

They then give up and accept defeat, without even throwing a punch. They have unknowingly, but willingly, accepted to have the rope round their necks.

People in this category, then with time, advance to perpetual moaners. Day in, day out, they do nothing else but sit around and moan about their circumstances, about how they have been set up. They blame everybody for their predicament. Their general outlook is that all they can do is just while away time and wait. They await the arrival of the man with the knife. The man with the knife will cut them free of this bondage. He will cut away the rope.

But then, how is one sure that the man expected to cut away the rope will do so without cutting a major neck artery? Death is instantaneous if he does. Or how is one, on the other hand, sure that the man who one hopes to be kind enough to cut the rope is not one of those creatures that feed on blood, on human blood? If that is the case, then what better place is there in the body to effortlessly suck blood from if not the arteries and veins of the neck? And yet this is the part of the body that our victimised friend delivers on a platter. They queue up waiting to be delivered, without having thought about, reflected upon or reckoned with the potential price they would be expected to pay to be cut free.

2

They don't have to like you

2.1   At the beginning

You have a problem.

At least that is what many kids, especially in the West, will want to make you believe.

They will try to make you feel bad.

They will call you names. The names would be different from the one we gave you. They are not nice names.

I cannot guarantee that things will completely normalise when you become an adult. It is likely to just be different. Things are unlikely to be said to your face any more, but I'm sure you should be fine by then.

I expect you to be in the position to laugh at such people's ignorance by then. Not openly... of course not, but deep inside, to yourself. I would not have done something right if you don't.

You were different from the outset, and this will always be the case. I hope it helps to bear in mind that you are the product of a wonderful union, a deep affection.

Whatever experience you have as a result of your looks should, however, be no excuse for any irrational action or behaviour, for you are better than that. You are your father's son.

2.2   Be yourself

My hope is that you believe so much in yourself that it wouldn't matter much to you what your peers say about you. You are simply too strong for whatever they say or do. This is because what they think makes absolutely no difference. What matters is what you think, what you believe.

My son, it's all a mind thing.

I am not saying to you – be arrogant. No, never. What I am saying is that you should always walk with your head high and that you should not allow yourself to be intimidated.

Smile a lot. This works both ways. There is something both disarming and infectious about having a smile on your face most of the time. It rubs off and makes you appear less threatening, but approachable. Smiling a lot is also healthier for you. So, smile a lot. Appear, and be, happy. It starts with the mind. If you believe and tell yourself enough, while constantly reminding yourself of why you should be happy, then you are likely to be, and to appear, happy.

Above all though, be and remain yourself, no matter the circumstances.

If the people around you cherish you enough, then they should be happy to accept you as you are. If they do not or cannot, then they have a problem, not you. Aim to be loved and appreciated, but realise that your life does not depend on it. Do not therefore go too much out of your way so as to make others appreciate you. You will expend too much energy doing that, and for what? What would you have gained? The truth is that no matter what you do, there will always be people who will criticise you and be of the view that things should have been done differently. People will, within reason, need to learn to love you the way you are. Be, therefore, in other words, true to yourself.

Even when you make the effort to be appreciated by others it should not be for just anybody. It should be for that person who has shown that they are worth, in whichever way, the trouble. The tendency is that if you push, and overdo things in order to please, the people you do it for could make you believe what you want to believe, but will still say what they really think about you behind your back. You certainly do not need that. You can also not please all the people all of the time. It will be a major mistake to even try. I will go further and suggest that something is likely wrong if you are indeed succeeding in doing that.

Again, remember that if you succeed in making everybody else happy, one person is guaranteed not to be happy – that person is you.

2.3   Start with loving yourself

I will not lie and say it is the easiest thing to do, but your best bet is to do all you can to avoid the temptation of going to unnecessary lengths to make others like you. You:

- do not have to.
- have no reason to.

It will not work.

Loving oneself is all easy actually, depending on how one looks at it. In the process of loving yourself, you're fully in control and it all starts with you. Here it all starts with you loving yourself. Note that I did not say like yourself, but love yourself. The first challenge is that nobody should love you as much as you love yourself. You should, put differently, love yourself the most. Make yourself your best friend and be ready to stick with this friend no matter what. It might sound odd, big-headed, and a bit counter-intuitive, but your love for yourself should know no bounds.

There will be good times ahead, and there will equally be bad times. You, and you alone, will find ways of navigating your way through all of such times. The truth is that it all starts with you. People around you can be supportive and understanding, but the only face you see when you look into the mirror, be it when you're crying or when you're laughing, will always be yours. You'd better get used to, love, and nourish the person behind that face.

There will be periods you will be ill, and periods you will be healthy.

There will be times you will think that nobody loves you, and times you will wonder why everybody wants to be your friend.

There will be times you will wonder, why am I going through this? but get no answer. There will be times when it will all be cold, very cold out there; when you will need to keep yourself warm… or freeze.

It is all part of this journey called life. You will meet all sorts of people along the way. Many will come and go. What will, however, remain a constant is you, sorting yourself out. You have to be able to stand strong and to be able to weather the bad storms, to pick yourself up when you fall. Others could help or attempt to do so, but the truth ultimately, my son, is that it is, and will be, down to you.

2.4   Life as a party

Imagine life sometimes like a party, a big party. You are the host, so the party is taking place at your own home. The house is full of people. There is enough to eat and drink. There is laughter, mixed with music in the air. Everybody is happy. You wouldn't want to go to bed, but actually wish that this fun would not come to an end; that it would go on forever and never stop. The reality of the situation is that the party is bound to come to an end, and will come to an end. It is programmed to happen. Refusing to go to bed will not stop it. Fighting sleep, in order to get as much as possible from the excitement will also not stop the party from coming to an end. Being extra nice to your guests and even bribing them will not make a lot of difference either. OK, they might stay on if you pay them, but you must also realise that the party is over anyway. The truth is that if they stay on, they're at this point in time no longer staying because it is such a nice party, or because they are your friends and want to stay by you. No, not at this point in time. If they still stay on, then it is more likely because of what they are getting from you. That is, however, not so bad.

What you must additionally realise is that if your guests all eventually leave, not only will you be left alone, all by yourself, you will also have to clear out all the mess they caused, since the party was carried out in your house. So, you need to have factored that in.

You have to be able to clear the mess after the party is over and you're all alone. By this time, the fair-weather friends, and there would be a lot of them, would all have gone. Think about it. Can you see yourself, can you imagine yourself coping? Or do you think you would crumble?

What I am talking about is more obvious with the rich and famous, the stars. Especially those who strike it very big. Almost every day becomes a party, a big party. They do not have a shortage of guests. They pay handsomely for the company of these guests and are, all of a sudden, seen as role models, so people will be stepping on each other's heads to attract their attention. The sad bit is that our friend, the star, begins to confuse this show with reality. It all gets blurred and the small line that differentiates fantasy from reality becomes even thinner. To everyone else, other than him, it remains just a show though. He is, however, oblivious to this, until disaster strikes – when he is left, home alone, to clear his personal troubles. He is likely to then find that he cannot cope.

Don't get me wrong, having people around you is important. It is in fact so important that you should make it a point of duty to aim to continuously increase the circle of the number of people you're in contact with. In life, you cannot do it all alone, it will be misleading to think you should attempt to. But always have at the back of your mind that it is you, and nobody else, who will have to find ways of bringing things back to normal when the music stops playing. It is your party – this point should be clear at all times.

If the above is well understood, then how much time (especially time), money, concern, afterthought do you think you can afford to spend on making people like you? How much? Well, you would have to decide.

2.5   Life is too long for a selfish person

I am not asking you to be selfish or self-centred. No. Selfish people are normally very short-sighted in terms of attitude. They cannot see beyond their noses and they also lack the ability to think mid to long-term. All they are programmed to see is immediate gain, and they forfeit all else in the pursuit of that. Their vocabulary is directly or indirectly made up of two words – me and now.

No, I cannot ask you to be self-centred, because you give in order to get. It then follows that he who does not give, gets nothing and that the more one gives, the more one is likely to receive. Although what has to be given does vary, it's generally that simple.

I can also not ask you not to be considerate, especially of other people's feelings. It will not always be easy, but the aim should be to do unto others as you would want done unto you. You should always be able to have a clear conscience, during and after your dealings with your fellow human beings. You have nothing to either fear or worry about if you can consistently do this. I will ask you to go even further than that and be nice to others; just be sure to stop at the point of being nice to them in order to be accepted or loved, for this is bound to fail.

Just as was stated by Wilson Mizner, that one should 'be nice to people on your way up because you'll meet the same people on your way down', life could be an exciting roller coaster of a ride. Life does not travel in straight lines, so yours is bound to be made up of several twists and a couple of ups and downs. That much is to be expected. Your best chance is therefore to think long-term. So, take things into perspective and, in both your reflection and your planning, concentrate on the big picture. So the reasoning, especially during rough patches, should therefore be in the lines… 'despite the temporal setback I'm going through at the moment, the general trajectory of my life has been and will remain, upwards and towards my long-term goal'. I wish I had better news than to tell you that you will unfortunately need to remind yourself of the last quote, which you might also need to repeat to yourself on a couple of occasions – after life has dealt you one of the expected several blows.

So think long-term, also in your interaction with others. Therefore, except in extreme cases, where certain lines have been crossed, I would say you should avoid hastily shutting people out completely from your life.

2.6   Remain different

The talk is about being different. Being different has nothing to do with being good or bad, it just means you're unique – which is great. The people who have problems with you being different are the others, people around. They are certainly the people you need not worry about.

Some people pride themselves in being able to very quickly analyse other people, and that they can decide within seconds of meeting somebody if they like that person or not. In order to do this, they often have to depend on a mixture of instinct and their past experiences to help them make such decisions. They make use of experiences they have made in the past as control, and then match what they're seeing now with what they know or have come across in the past – they then make a decision about the person in front of them based on how the two pictures match. It is a matter of approaching the unknown with the known.

Question then, however, is, what do such people then do when they're faced by people or situations that are completely new – so new that they have nothing stored up in the archives of their memory to make references to? Do they stop to think and reflect more on things, as one would expect them to? Of course not. What they do is more the opposite. They are, in such situations, even quicker to jump to conclusions. It is in the nature of human beings to follow the path of least resistance. So in this instance, they allow their brain to do a quick scan. The brain of course finds nothing. The person, however, believes that they have to make immediate decisions – do they like this person or not; should they or can they trust this person or not? – but the brain is just not capable of supplying the necessary information. It is one of the basic modes, in which the brain also operates, when it has the capability to work like a very advanced computer which relies on stored data in order to know what the next step would be. When this reference point is missing (and since it is part of the survival instinct for beings to strive to protect themselves from harm) the person in question would force the brain to jump to a conclusion to fill in the missing link. Only problem is that the reached conclusion is here not based on facts, but on feelings, or hearsay, or an article in the local newspaper or even a documentary on TV.

I want you to bear these points in mind when some stranger approaches you in a funny way, with some pre-formed opinion about you, that neither you nor I know the origin of. An opinion we both know is wrong and has nothing to do with reality. It would be an error, which would additionally motivate them even further, to take the views of such people seriously. It will only cost you precious energy and distract you from focusing on the really important things in life. Don't waste time on such people or their opinions, for what do they know?

You are different, my son. This is something to be proud of. In fact, strive to be different, enjoy it, nurse and nurture it. Being different is a wonderful gift and I completely fail to see how something so good could be turned into something to be ashamed of. Think of it as being unique. You are an original copy, no imitation. Few things can put you on a better footing than being different. Enjoy it and make the best out of it.

Do not join the bandwagon. Actually, keep away from the crowd if getting too close will rub off and make you be like them.

Do what you think you have to do; then muster the courage and stick to it. That is the stuff successful people are made of.

This will be a good time to bring to your notice a letter Abraham Lincoln was said to have written to his son's teacher, which I believe is readily available online. See if you can find, and read it.

2.7   On appearance and race

People always need those to look down on, while most people need someone to look up to.

One of the worst things that could happen to a person is to be entirely on their own. Most things, in such a case, would not make sense. We normally need others in order to feel good in and about ourselves. People often feel good or bad in themselves relative to how they think others feel in themselves or how they think they are seen by others.

We therefore tend to wear our best clothes when we are about to leave the house, and dress down on our return. We also dress better while at home if expecting visitors. Left to themselves, most people would remain dressed in nightclothes for most of the day, if they do not have plans to leave the house or meet with others.

Your friends would similarly mostly feel great in themselves if people around them were able to admire (and possibly be envious of) their nice trainers and designer clothes. Adults similarly buy the nicest cars, want to live in the biggest houses and spend exorbitant sums of money on other perceived pleasures of life to make others know how well they are doing. Somebody who lives alone on a remote island is less likely to worry about these things. There would be no one to show off to.

Part of the point is that people tend to need others at least as a form of reference point. How good or bad, how sad or happy they feel about themselves is usually in relation to how they perceive things to be with those around them. You've certainly heard the saying about the one-eyed man being king in the land of the blind. How do you think the same one-eyed person would feel in a land of two-eyed people? You answered, "like a lower-class person" when I asked you the exact same question, and you could be right.

People generally want to feel good and special. It is how they go about doing this that is different. What does it for a lot of people, especially those with low self-confidence, is the imagination that human beings are on various rungs of some form of ladder in society. It is, in order to make things easier when thinking this way, common to group people together. What you are most likely to come across is that people are grouped together based on how they look, or their race. What tends to happen is that people with different tones of skin colour get put on various rungs of the hierarchical ladder. It seems to make those who think they are higher up feel better in themselves.

Yes, human beings could be that primitive. Despite all the advances in technology and how far the human race has come, you will still find that some absurd things persist and continue to be propagated by humans. The tone of a person's skin pigment, the shade of which the person has absolutely no say in, is often allowed to play an unimaginably massive role in the person's life, and in many instances, determines the person's fate – just like that.

The same thing applies to appearance. While it is true that the first thing people see is how a person looks, the problem is that most people are unable to look beyond someone's physical appearance. What you then find is that the same mistake of remaining fixated on looks ends up playing a disproportionate role in terms of how one gets treated. People tend to lack the patience and the inclination to consider other attributes others have but instead often allow both their vision and attitude to be clouded by looks.

Now, anybody is free to think what he or she wants about themselves. Allowing the way others decide to think, and carry themselves, to affect you is, however, a different matter. It is ultimately your decision if you want to accept the position, in society, that others think is where you fit or belong. Would you really want another person's way of thinking to determine who you are and what your capabilities and limitations are? Would you really want to do them such a favour, or would you rather think 'you can think and believe whatever you want, but I know I am better than that'?

3

Learn early to say no

3.1   Again, love yourself

It is normally easier to go with the flow, as they say. You that way do not stand out, you don't become a target; nobody troubles you and you trouble nobody. You're just one of them, a face in the crowd. You're thus guaranteed friends. You're also not perceived a 'troublemaker', a dissident. The likelihood instead is that you would be seen as 'one of us'. It is hence the easiest and most convenient thing to blend in as much as possible, to not be overtly conspicuous. Well, easiest could be most convenient, but certainly not best.

Saying no is one of the most difficult things to do, at least until you get used to it. Like with all things, you get better with practice.

The very first step in the process of getting to be able to say no is – you have to like yourself. You have to like yourself more than anybody else does. This is absolutely the number one step. I have tried to show you how much I love you, even though it is not always easy for me to do this all the time. I can tell you that there is hardly anybody in the whole wide world who will love you as much as I do. I look at you and I see a part of me. I see a continuation. There is no break in transmission. It is like going full circle, starting at point A and ending exactly at point A. My love for you is unconditional. I will love you in good and bad times.

I want you, however, to know that in order to be able to learn how to say no, you have to love yourself more than anybody else loves you, including how much I love you. That is how much you have to love yourself, never less. This is certainly the starting point.

As was discussed, you need to realise that you are very special. Treat and carry yourself so, with a lot of dignity, but without being unnecessarily arrogant and too full of yourself. A fine line divides these two, you would need to find and tread on it carefully. Do the things you do and say the things you say because you are special and because you're you. It is the person who does not have a lot of self worth who feels compelled to do things the way every other person does, or the way they're supposed to. They think they have to 'fit in'.

3.2   Then you have to believe, in yourself

Next to loving yourself, is the fact that you have to believe in yourself. This is not as easy as it sounds though. It is easy to believe in yourself when everything is moving fine and everybody is happy with you. The difficult part is believing in yourself when things become tough and people around you are not as happy with you. When you think everybody is against you that's when believing in yourself becomes difficult, but crucial. So, what you are aiming for is a complete belief in yourself. The level of self-belief has to be unshakeable and unapologetic.

These two things – unconditional love of yourself and a very strong belief in yourself – go hand in hand if you want to be able to say no. Remember these two requirements by thinking of them as the sandwich. These two things are like the two slices of bread on the outside of the sandwich. The middle part of the sandwich, with all the good things like cheese, butter, and sometimes fish and vegetables, is like saying no. The good stuff in the sandwich are kept in place by the two slices of bread. Without the slices of bread, there can be no sandwich.

The two slices of bread that hold the sandwich in place are, in your case, deep profound love of yourself and an unshakeable belief in yourself.

Feel sorry for the person who depends on others to tell them how good they are, for they will not go very far.

Learn early to have the courage to stand and fight or to turn your back on the crowd and go your own way if you feel you have to, or if you think you're right. Few things could be more fulfilling. You are, amongst other things, forced to discover and better understand yourself by so doing. You will also soon find out that you will be forced to improvise and to think a lot along the way, especially as you will be walking through untrodden footpath. You will have to devise means of keeping on. Finding your own way, thus moving away from what everyone else does, would certainly appear very daunting initially, but I will tell you one thing – it is the stuff that ALL great people and geniuses are made of. They all have to deviate from the masses and do things differently. They never get to such levels by following the crowd. They somehow are able to muster the courage to do things their own way or to deviate completely from the crowd. It makes sense and is quite easy to understand if you really come to think about it – if you do what everyone else does, or expects you to do, you will certainly end up like every other person, or as everybody else wants you to be. What you would amount to would definitely not be much. You will be average, if anything at all.

I was there when your mother gave birth to you. I have watched you develop since then. I am convinced, from what I have seen of you, that you have what it takes, that you have the mental strength and that you can muster enough will and perseverance to excel and reach incredible heights in any venture you put your mind to. You can go all the way. Do not listen to the person who would, even in the subtlest way, suggest to you otherwise.

Believe what I am saying for I do not have a cause to want to deceive you. I do not have an ulterior motive, except maybe to see you succeed in life. And if you do believe me, then step out of the shadows and go for it, boldly.

> Come to the edge.
> We might fall.
> Come to the edge.
> It's too high!
> COME TO THE EDGE!
> And they came and he pushed and they flew…
>
> Christopher Logue (*Come to the Edge*)

3.3   So what is no? (Like cat and dog)

I will now tell you a few things about the word no.

No is the complete opposite of another important word called yes.

You have always said you prefer cats to dogs so I will use the two animals to show you the difference between yes and no.

I want you to see saying yes as a dog and saying no as a cat for my illustration. The reason will become clear shortly.

You always say that you find dogs a bit dumb, so I am sure you will understand.

Dog = Yes
Has no own opinion.
Always does what people around think it should. Quickly responds to "Sit", "Come", "Go".
Very predictable, hence hardly capable of causing surprises.
Has little self-respect. Can you remember the dog we saw the other day eating human faeces?
Mostly need to be walked by the owner.

Cat = No
Certainly has own opinion.
Cares less about what people around think.
Has a lot of self-respect and pride. Will certainly not eat faeces.
Does not even eat *just any* cat food since it is very selective.
Certainly does not need to be walked. Will leave the house, and come back, when it pleases.

Don't get me wrong, yes is an important word that we need very often. It is actually one of the most used words. The problem is that it is overused. It was a strong and powerful word a long time ago. But like the dog, it has become over-tamed into a very timid, unsure and very dependent domestic animal that is often lacking in self-confidence.

I know you are intelligent, so you will be wondering, "Well, if it is so nice and cool to say no, why is everybody not doing it?", especially as you will come across your friends saying yes to everything and everybody.

Well, one of the reasons is that people now say yes when they mean to say no.

It is easier.

It is politer.

It makes them feel more accepted.

They don't want to hurt the other person.

They think it is the only way of belonging. They think they will otherwise not have friends to play with.

They are afraid.

The word no is so important I would want you to start using it more and as early as possible.

So later, when your friends tell you to come and play football, even though you have not finished your school homework, you know what to say.

Continue practising the use of this word and I promise you it will be easier to say no, when you have to, with time – especially when you become able to express yourself more diplomatically, so that instead of bluntly saying no, you say something like "I would like to, but …".

I have to mention that several people have adopted a different version of saying no, since no one can say yes all of the time. While I'm not saying you should (or should not) do the same, I am asking you to be aware of this. A lot of people find it easier to say yes when they know deep inside that they mean no. So even though they say yes, they know already that they will never carry out what they said yes to. For them, saying yes is another, less confrontational way, of saying no. What they then do is to say yes but then later not make any effort to do what they said they would. They can, in other words, conveniently allow the promise to do something 'escape' their mind. They could decide to 'forget', believing this approach to guarantee better results. See what suits you, but either way…

3.4   Say no

Saying no means not doing things the way everybody else is doing things, or expects you to. It is best when you can say no, not because you want to prove a point, but because you believe, and are convinced that you are right. Let your no be based on what you are

convinced of. Like I said, it is a difficult thing to do, but it is much easier – in fact the trick is – to be sure of why you're saying no, and then stick to it. There is a difference between what I am saying and being headstrong or stubborn. Stubborn people believe – no, they are convinced – that things should go the way they want it, even when they are wrong. They're effectively also saying no, but doing that because they think they have to prove a point. This is usually a different form of silliness.

The main problem you will face is the reaction of the people around you, especially your friends. They will think and say strange things about you when you say no where everybody else is saying yes. This is where our first two points (which are?) become very important. You simply cannot cope with the negative reaction you will definitely receive when you say no, if you cannot love yourself and believe in yourself enough. You will be like that sandcastle we once built too close to the water at the beach. The first little wave comes along, and whoosh, you're gone.

Be consistent and aim to be an expert at being able to say no by the time you are an adult. This is a powerful tool, which has to be used with care, and only when necessary, for it to be effective. Do not be tempted to say no when you don't have to, or to say no when what you meant was yes. This weakens the effectiveness of your no, for how would the other person actually know that your no is really no?

As an adult, people, and society, expect you to be able to say no when you have to. It is seen as your fault if you're not able to.

You need to know when you should draw a line and say "I will get to this point, but not further!" Nobody is going to look at you and say, "I think he has suffered enough, maybe we should leave him alone now". No, they won't. As long as you don't show or say that you've had enough, believe me, nothing will change. People will still be going at you, left, right and centre. It is natural that human beings tend to want to look after themselves first, it is another survival instinct. They will also not be able to feel what you are feeling, certainly not the way you are feeling it. You have to show and tell them what you are feeling and how strongly you are feeling it. You also have to let them know that because what they expect you to do is either so painful and is hurting so much, is so uncomfortable, so against your principles and what you stand for, so uncalled for, such a waste of time, so insulting to you, or so disrespectful that there is no way you would be able to go on. Just say NO! It is as simple as that. The initiative can only come from you, and it is also left for you to be able to convey to them how STRONG your no is. If you do a good job at being able to convey things the way they are, others will IMMEDIATELY understand. They are mostly not stupid. Now, I will not lie to you and tell you that this is going to be easy; no, it won't be. This is the reason you would, amongst other things, need a large measure of courage, self-belief and self-worth to pull it through. If you are convinced, after several efforts, that you have done a good job, but that the other person/others still do not appreciate your point of view, or see things from your perspective, then you know what to do. If they would, despite all your effort, still not accept no for an answer, then it would be one of the rare occasions when you would have to leave everything behind and RUN! Dissociate yourself as much as possible and run for dear life. For what it means is that

they do not have your interests at heart. If you do not take the steps to save yourself, you will drown, you will get crushed.

The worst bit is that the people concerned might not even appreciate the fact that they are the cause of your predicament. So, it might have to be a case of trying to save yourself first, and then conveying the reason for your action later – assuming it still remains unclear.

3.5   Other forms of no

There will also be lots of times when you have to say no, but this time around not to people, but to circumstances. Do not shy away from such situations, which are bound to come, when you should stand up and shout "No, I cannot take this any more!" In which case, you again, don't just say it, but do it – do not take it any more. Change something, do something.

3.6   It depends on you

What *you accept* to tolerate will reflect in situations and circumstances of your whole life. In other words, what you get out of life depends on what you accept and expect you are worthy of. You have to set the standards of your expectations of yourself and that of others towards you. If you tolerate and accept disrespect, for instance, that's what you get. If you tolerate being used by others and give the impression you're OK with this, that's what happens. It is not unusual for people, shortly after they meet someone new, to push all boundaries to get a sense of how much nonsense the person they just met will accept, hence how far they can safely go. If, say with the intention of being nice to this person, you become too accommodating and allow yourself to be pushed around and for too much dirt to be thrown at your face, then you cannot later complain about the consequences, for you would have demonstrated (even if unconsciously) acceptable standards. You would have given a good idea of what you would accept and what you wouldn't. It's all down to you, even though it could all happen so quickly you could end up not realising you were the one who set the bar, the standards. The tendency could then be to blame others and, say, accuse them of pushing you about, or of being exploitative. Well, the good (or bad, depending on how you would prefer to see it) news is that you actually communicated your preference to them earlier. So it is not their fault, but entirely (to 100%) yours.

3.7   It is *always* down to you

I know this point has been mentioned before, but will be emphasised a few more times, due to its importance; one of the most critical lessons, which takes a while to fully sink in, is that of finally accepting that you are ultimately responsible. So, the sooner you finally accept that it is at the end of the day down to you in terms of what you do or don't do; how you respond or don't respond to whatever is done or said to you, the more of a better person you are going to be.

The other person can provoke you, insult you or tease you all they want. There will always be some window period between their action and your response and how long this period is could vary, but what you finally decide to do then boils down to you. How you handle the situation, how you respond (or not respond) is going to be 100% (nothing less) down to you.

There is, by way of example, hardly a better way of illustrating this point than by asking you to reflect on what you would do in the following scenario. In several so-called developing countries, people need to have a shower outside the house, usually in a small outbuilding, which would normally have low walls in some areas. What tends to happen is that one would put one's clothes, soap and towel on this lower part of the wall while having a shower, as provision is normally not made for leaving such items, which would get soaked if left on the floor. So, imagine that you are enjoying an afternoon shower on a very sunny day in one of such outbuildings when all of a sudden, you realise that your clothes and towel have disappeared. You look over the lower wall quickly to see a person you had previously been warned about of having some form of mental disturbance running away with these items! Horror grips you on quickly realising the implication of what has just happened. The question, my son, is, what would you do? The items taken away belong to you, there is no question about that. So, you have the right to do all you can to get your stuffs back. Bearing that in mind, what would you still do? Would you, for instance, immediately bolt out yourself, since you calculate you would run faster than the poor soul, and run as fast as you can towards him? Would you, in other words, immediately do everything within your power to retrieve your items as soon as humanly possible and inform anyone who would listen (or pay attention) that that is exactly what you intend to do? You might be right, but take a moment to think about how the scenario would come across to an observer, especially one who is not aware of the whole story, or your perspective. Take things a bit further and, let's assume you dash after this person completely naked (in fact, still partially covered in soapy water), while screaming at the top of your voice that they should immediately return your items, that they have no right to take them and at the same time reminding them of the possible actions you intend to otherwise take, and how you could break their legs if you caught up with them. So, imagine you two have now run up to the front of the main building and are seen by complete strangers; you know, passers-by. What the strangers would see is a man who is quite dishevelled and dressed in tattered clothes being pursued by a completely naked man who can hardly keep his eyes open due to the pain in his eyes from the soapy water and who is screaming and raving at the top of his lungs.

How are these strangers likely to interpret this amusing scenario? Will they, when recounting the story to others later, not report how they saw two mad people running after each other earlier in the day? If you think about it, would you blame them for coming to such a conclusion?

The take-home message here is that how others behave towards you should ideally not fully determine how you react or respond. Their behaviour should, in other words, not be an excuse and should not be seen to justify your behaviour or reaction. Be wary therefore of attempting to immediately match cause with an effect, an action with a reaction or an eye for an eye.

3.8   Dr P

I once worked with an immigrant colleague, Dr P. Her family came from one of the war-torn countries and she had seen a lot of pain and suffering in her life. She, other than for her very unwell mother, who she looked after alone, did not have other family members around. She also had a couple of other issues, and they all had an impact on her. These problems affected the quality of her work and her interaction with others at work. Some of her actions also raised questions about her judgement. It did not take that long for a lot of animosity to be generated towards her. People were disrespectful towards her and did not seem to think twice about the content of what they said to her, or, to some extent, how she was treated. It was not a good sight to behold.

Her understanding of the best way to handle the situation was to hide away, avoid confrontational situations and hope the whole thing would lose momentum and die a natural death. This of course did not work, and matters instead got more out of hand.

The environment was, on its own, busy and stressful enough and people were seeking outlets for their frustrations and also for scapegoats. She blindly walked into the role of a sacrificial lamb, and was blamed for all that was wrong at the unit. It was a complex and messy situation. When it became clear I was not making progress with being protective and it was also not in her best interest to do otherwise, I had to suggest that it was best for her to go, and start afresh elsewhere.

It took a while to sink in, but she eventually handed in her notice. While talking about it before she left, she could not stop expressing a deep sense of relief she was by then experiencing. She further wondered why she could not have done it on her own, without support, and then opened up about how she would usually accept being trampled upon in the past, which I saw as a fair question to ask oneself.

3.9   Pick your fights

My son, do not shy away from a fight, but on the other hand pick your fights very carefully. Without underestimating your opponent, avoid starting a fight you are unlikely to win and as Mike said to Bill in *The Golden Amulet*, by Mark Engebretson, "Don't draw unless you're ready and willing to shoot, and don't shoot unless you're ready and willing to kill. If you're not willing to do that, don't pull it. The reason you have it is to defend yourself and if you feel you have to pull it, it's because the other man is a threat. Once he sees it, he won't hesitate and you'll be dead, regardless of your intentions when you pulled it. There's no going back from a killing. You can't say, 'Hey, wait a minute, I didn't mean it'. It's too late then. That's why you have to be sure". The truth remains the same and you should, in your case, endeavour not to start a fight you are unlikely to win. Pick your fights, and your opponents, with care. It is not cowardice, but one of the important rules of war.

This, unfortunately, also partly explains what goes on during bullying. Bullies can only try to intimidate and terrorise those they think they can get away with such an attitude with. They still carefully pick who they harass or mess with. The quiet, softly spoken one, who maybe looks different and also has no friends then becomes an easy target... except they can find a way of striking back, which then forces the bully to disappear and search out a new victim.

3.10   Take home

The truth is that NOBODY can seriously and considerably cause you emotional harm or distress except if you sign up to it and accept for this to happen. As it cannot occur without your permission, you would have to allow them. In other words, whether they succeed or not is ultimately down to you. You really have to allow them to get away with whatever it is. Putting yourself in the very situation, and not doing something, or enough, to either protect yourself or change things, is a direct (not indirect) way of giving your consent for the way you ultimately get treated.

4

Heaven can wait

4.1   We're talking about life here on Earth

The good, or maybe bad, thing about heaven and hell is that I personally have not seen anybody who went, saw and came back to tell the story. There are at least three reasons for this – things are either too good up there; terrible; or it is a simple case of no way back. The reason why people don't come back when they die notwithstanding, the idea of what happens when one dies remains a matter of opinion.

This opinion is largely influenced by:

which part of the world one comes from;

the kind of teachings that one received, especially as a child;

the impact of religion;

experiences that one has gone through in life;

the person's need to believe in something;

and some reports of near-death incidents and subsequent accounts reported to have been given by such people.

Who knows, maybe one day we would have an answer to what really happens when one dies, but for now this event that is bound to take place, since everybody must die, remains a mystery.

Is it then not troubling that there are, however, people who lay so much emphasis on where they would go when they die that they allow this question to have too strong an influence on their daily thoughts and actions? The issue could be important, but can it really, in terms of priority, be as crucial as some people would want to make you believe?

I fail to understand why someone would worry so much about what they know so little about and that is so distant, so far away; especially if this is done to the detriment of improving their life **now.** Sometimes one wonders if it would not make more sense to leave the dead to worry about heaven, while we, the living, worry about life.

4.2   Talking of heaven, whose heaven?

An interesting point is the position of most of the population of the so-called developing countries in the issue of heaven from a religious point of view. The idea about the existence of heaven or hell is, to the best of my knowledge, foreign to such countries. This manner of thinking simply did not exist, until these countries were visited by the Europeans. It was these Europeans who introduced this concept of heaven and hell. It is then quite remarkable that the indigenes could turn around and become such strong believers in this concept about the existence of heaven and hell.

It is similar to what is happening in other areas of life of the inhabitants of such countries. They have abandoned, apparently without questioning, their ways of thinking and their religion, for beliefs that, as far as I am concerned, make no sense to them whatsoever.

It is interesting that what used to be the culture and way of life of the Europeans has largely become so adopted and accepted by people who then turn around and see their own tradition as not being good enough any more. It is, indeed, interesting, but sad. I am not sure about the argument for not seeing things this way, the way they are. So, we end up with a scenario whereby someone who is European is fascinated, just as I am, by the tradition of my country and its people, and would love to experience a part of it but is usually not quite able to do that. This is because what obtains in my culture is seen as not as important as how it would have been done in the culture of the Westerner. Meaning that the way things are done in the West is perceived as better, just because it was packaged and presented through Christianity.

The problem is that topics such as religion are no-go areas. Like taboos, you're not allowed to think of them, not to mention discussing them. You just have to accept things the way they are. Commenting on, not to talk of questioning, such beliefs has very successfully been portrayed as being equivalent to questioning the presence, and hence, the existence of God. A blasphemy. If you do not carry out a church wedding, then God has not blessed your marriage, so you are committing sin and would therefore go to hell when you die.

I just often wonder; what about my forefathers, those that lived before Christianity was introduced? Does it then mean that the way they did things was not correct? So, since none of my forefathers or great-forefathers carried out church weddings, and if the theory is to go by, does it not then mean that they, and we their offspring, who are the result of such unholy relationships, would all end up rotting in hell? Who has the right to make such a strong decision about another person's culture and tradition? Or, on the other hand, what would make a people come to so strongly believe and accept the idea that what they have, and which was handed down from generation to generation to them, was suddenly not now good enough? It's a pity.

It is similar to the notion that one has to go to church every Sunday, no matter what. If you do not go to church every week, then you're the worst sinner imaginable and you are bound to go to hell as well. It is very important to go to church on Sunday (or Saturday in some cases) and act 'holy' during the church service. You would, if you're Catholic, of course, have confessed your sins and then had them forgiven a day or two before the church service. You would that way have done your duty. You are then allowed to go back afterwards to your normal ways and continue to commit your sins again. Not exactly, but that's what happens. Don't get me wrong, I was born into a Catholic family but still see some of what obtains in the churches (including the Catholic Church) difficult to follow.

I've always thought that if half of the people who visit places of worship every week (or even daily in some cases) were to practise half of what they learnt at such places, then the world would be a much better place to be. There would for instance be no corruption. My belief is that going to church every Sunday, for instance, serves a mixture of different functions for the people. It has, amongst other things, become more of a social event than anything else although most people still believe that going to church every week guarantees their going to heaven. It is also one of those activities that societies that practise them have unquestionably accepted as standard. Anything else is not good enough and should be well explained. The people have accepted that and have unconsciously agreed that this decision is never to be questioned.

It sure is quite amazing to what length people go in order to safeguard their place in the paradise called heaven. A place from which they have not seen anybody who has successfully done a return trip.

You will also hear of people of other religious backgrounds who commit all sorts of atrocities following promises of some wonderful encounters in paradise, when they die. You will have to decide on how rational that idea is.

It does not cease to amaze me how much time people freely throw away in the name of religious activity attendance. They have so little value for the most precious thing in their lives, time, that they do not seem to mind how much of it they get rid of. You have instances where people attend religious activities on an almost daily basis, where they don't have full-time employment, or most of their weekends are used up for engagement in such activities, where they work during the week. They also seem to forget that God is said to be everywhere and not just confined to the four walls of a religious building. So instead of utilising their time to better themselves, also by improving their skills, or learning new ones, most of their time is instead used 'worshipping' God. What I see in most such cases is a set of people who seem to believe they are entitled to preferential treatment from God, purely because they use as much time as possible singing God's grace. It's difficult to see how God will enormously reward someone who has in most cases demonstrated an inability to excel independently but to instead live on the hope of being provided with blessings on a platter, despite the absolute lack of initiative.

4.3   To get to heaven, you would have to die first

There is a big difference between somebody doing something because of the type of legacy that they want to leave behind when they die, and someone doing something because:

   a) they think they have to make the people around them happy;
   b) they feel compelled by society to do things they are convinced do not make sense; and worse still;
   c) because they want to go to heaven when they **die**.

Note that die is emphasised above. The interesting thing is that people often forget that even if you believe in the existence of heaven you would have to die first before you can talk about if you qualify to go to heaven or not. The believing aspect is just not enough. Many people, however, do not want to die, yet are very determined to go to heaven. Don't ask me, because I honestly do not know how that would work.

They want something, but they are not ready to do something

for it. They don't want to put their neck on the line. Why should they, when big brother is going to sort them out anyway?

Instead of all the time and energy spent on what might as well be called an illusion, why not spend half the time on what makes sense **now**? Why not invest the time and energy into what is certain, and that is the reality? Would it not be better to take the initiative and do something while we still live and can influence things?

The reality we have to face is that nobody will do it for us. Why would even God do so if we don't want it enough?

There are those who somehow believe that they do not have to do a lot because God will take care of them. I wonder if you could think about it this way though; God created everybody, right? If you believe that, as I am sure you do, then please think about it and tell me why you think God should take care of some people more than others? If I showed your sibling that I love him more than I love you, how do you think you would feel? God has also endowed us with the resources to make the maximum use of all he has created. Except for those who have obvious handicaps, there is really not a lot of excuse. But even talking about handicaps, there are two men who have been able to very successfully shake up the music industry. They are both very unique and peculiar men. Though black and blind, Ray Charles and Stevie Wonder were able to get to the pinnacle of being musicians at times in history when it was very difficult to know which was a greater sin – to be black or to be blind.

Would it not be reasonable to imagine that God would help us human beings equally, being the impartial God that he is? On what basis should God assist us more than our neighbour, or our enemy for that matter, who is incidentally more hard-working than we are? Would that really be a fair thing to do? I do not think so, and I am convinced God would not think so either. So, I hope you can see that it would not only be unfair for God to assist some people more than others, it would just not work. Because how would he decide on whom to love more? Should it be based on people's skin colour or on their age or based on their circumstances? You see, it wouldn't work.

I think that God will assist us equally. How far we are then able to go with the resources at our hands is therefore largely dependent on us, not God.

It is good to pray regularly, just as it is good to be God-fearing, but the reality is that that alone is not enough. You have to be able to back up your prayers with action. This is a peculiar attribute you will find in people who are very religious. One gets the impression that they believe that calling God's name in their times of need is enough. I don't know how one would just depend on that, for he is a fair God who would only act to bless our effort, with reward that is commensurate with our input. I can't imagine God being a partial God, who would effectively 'rob Peter to pay Paul'. Was it not in the Bible, the parable of the man who took from his less well-performing son to give to the son who seemed to know what to do with available resources (inheritance)?

To go to heaven, you should be ready to die first.

To reap, you should be ready to first of all sow. Manna, as far as I know, fell from heaven only in the Bible. It has not fallen again since.

4.4   Start with the end in mind

One of the ironies of life is that things become easier if you know where you're going and where you want to be. You need a sense of direction. Especially as you will be bombarded from all sides by distractions, you will definitely need a focus and this entails always having a list of preferences and priorities. You cannot afford to, as people say, go with the flow. It could be fun and less demanding in the short term, but long term you're losing out, big time.

This is what is easy to have problems with, for lots of people wonder how you can know where you're going without first being there. They lack the imagination. They are too afraid to think freely, to think like a child. A child's mind knows no boundaries – there are no limits, everything is possible. This remains the case until seeds of doubt are sown in the child's innocent mind. It starts with the child being constantly reminded to take small baby steps before attempting to walk normally; to initially hold the railing while they walk; to walk 'properly' before they attempt to run; to stop blabbing and only attempt to sing after they've mastered the art of speaking. They're constantly reminded of the consequences of carefully adhering to expected developmental milestones; that they are bound to injure themselves should they do things differently. And what happens when they, in their excitement ("Oh Mummy, Daddy, look I can run"), trip and have a nasty fall? They're scolded heavily: "What were you thinking? Did I not tell you to walk gently first and then take things easy? How many times do I have to explain this to you? Please be more careful and take it a step at a time. Don't make Daddy angry. Daddy has a lot of work to do." I wonder if there is any doubt that the child's wings are gradually clipped after a few such scenarios. They eventually land on the floor and adapt to being a 'good child'.

One of the first things you will learn as an adult or in the process of growing up is to be rational, to be realistic. These are important aspects of growing up but they also have strong disadvantages. There is, however, the danger of becoming too analytical, too grown up, which would mean blocking off a lot of the natural thinking processes. One would, funnily enough, think that one's method of thinking has become more advanced. This could be the case in many instances, but in most other cases, thinking becomes a more robotic and mechanical process mainly because people then unconsciously learn to think and make decisions based on past experiences. This is the way robots behave – they act based on the programme constructed by the person who manufactured them. They are fine as long as the issue at hand has been stored in their memory. They will not be able to perform if required to do so by circumstances which fall immediately outside the scope of their memory. They could know the definition, or even the interpretation of the word imagination; this word does, however, not exist for them.

Human beings without imagination will always be a step behind because they can only perform when following known footsteps. They are at their best after other people have cleared the way, after others have given them an idea of what to do, either by word of mouth or by action. This aspect of your being a child belongs to the characteristics I would ask you to keep and use, even as an adult. I will ask you to try and retain your ability to think freely, for there is massive power in this.

I must, however, mention, at this juncture, that there is something else, another way of following another person's footsteps, called mentorship, which is a brilliant idea. Having a good mentor could be one of the best things that could happen to you. This makes sense since the mentor has walked the path you want to walk. He or she knows where the surprises and ambushes are. Through the assistance of a mentor, your rate of achieving success could be changed to be in leaps and bounds because you benefit from your mentor's experiences. You thus on the one side become motivated, and on the other, avoid costly mistakes.

4.5   Sheep move as a herd

One of the main problems with being focused, especially at a young age, is the amount of ridicule you could be subjected to by your peers. They could see you as being old-fashioned and boring. Do not let that bother you, it should actually make you feel good about yourself and about what you're doing, or not doing as the case may be. One of the reasons you should be proud of yourself under such circumstances is that most human beings move in flocks, as a herd. The Lake District, where we've spent some time, is known for its sheep. You see them grazing in most parts of the district. They sit around for hours, munching grass and staring into space. They can be so absent-minded that one has to be careful not to knock them down while driving. There are instances when they stand in the middle of the road, and only slowly move (not run) away when you get out of the car and strongly indicate they should move out of the way.

Such a slow, mundane and passive lifestyle is all they know – spending all day munching away, oblivious of all the things going on around them. There's no hurry, no rush; why rush, hurry to where? Why make haste when the farmer (their owner) and his dog are surely going to come and direct them to where to spend the night?

Most people need to have the feeling that they are doing what everybody else is doing, is expecting them to do, or what everybody is happy with. It gives them a sense of security and belonging. It is moreover easier to just drift along with everybody else. This way, you're, amongst other things, guaranteed friends – since you all share the same views and aspirations.

Imagine the amount of resistance or even resentment that would go with trying to break away from this pattern of life. Think for a while how one of the sheep described earlier will be seen if it suddenly decides, after realising the futility of its existence, to break away from the herd and go, on its own, in an unknown and unexplored direction. Reflect for a moment on the amount of courage this 'crazy' sheep will need. The likelihood is that even the sheep closest to it would not be understanding. Worse is likely to be the reaction of its friends and peers. They, apart from thinking their friend has 'lost it' are bound to have a mixture of emotions. While some could be filled with worry for its welfare, others will be more antagonistic and think

"Who the hell does that fool actually think it is? Does it now think it is of better breed or class than the rest of us?" What tends to happen is that doing everything possible to avoid being in this position then ultimately means that most people would simply stick to the status quo and do all they can to avoid stepping out of the imaginary bond they believe binds them to those around them. This deep and very strong feeling then ultimately manifests as fear, predominantly that of failure, and extends to that of letting others down. They will then convince themselves that the idea of stepping out of line is indeed possibly crazy or of the making of the Devil – someone else would have to take the blame. It is easier to channel this outwards, rather than inwards, where it rightfully belongs.

The major problem with living this way, which shouldn't be surprising, is that you then end up like any other person. You become a Mister Average, or Mister Below-average – which is quite a shame considering all the wonderful things you were endowed with when you were created.

4.6   Reward yourself though for successes

There is no denying the fact that you need to once in a while reward yourself, especially after a good job well done. I remember my father always buying me presents each time I was the best pupil in my class. It was a superb type of motivation. I ended up receiving more things this way than during Christmas, which was the next time we generally had new clothes bought or sewn for us. So, I would in the same vein highly recommend celebrations and rewards after accomplishments. These are the things that often remain longer in our memory and which kind of prepare us for the next task.

What I, however, frown at is when one has no sense of direction and when fun and celebration is enjoyed to the point where they become second nature. The sun can sometimes shine before it rains, but it is always better when it rains before the sun shines.

You have a good head start if you learn to do these things at a tender age. I would therefore ask you to always keep your eyes on the larger picture, then to devise a plan that will take you where you want to be, and not to allow the mockery of your so-called friends to deter you.

Celebrate, be happy, have fun, buy yourself nice things if you can, especially to celebrate success. It is a way of patting yourself on the back for a job well done and those little treats would certainly help in keeping you motivated.

Do, however, reward yourself in moderation and make sure that the cost of the reward will not have a negative effect on the main project. If you have for instance invested money wisely, and it is yielding good interests, do not run out and buy yourself a present using part of the capital. When the interest earned becomes substantial, help yourself to a part of the interest and buy yourself or the people involved in the smooth running of the investment something – never with the capital.

4.7   Before you buy

Have you thought about the fact that each time you're spending money, you're making somebody somewhere richer, and yourself poorer of course? This is not supposed to mean that you should stop spending money, just something to bear in mind. It is no problem if you also have structures in place that would make you richer when others spend money as well. It is, however, not very enviable if all you do is make others richer. Worse still is if you're enriching other people who do not respect and cherish your enterprise. There are even instances where they are able to turn things round and want to make you feel grateful that you're 'allowed' to spend money on their products. This is achieved through good marketing. This is why prominent people like football stars and successful musicians are paid large sums of money to appear on television and in magazines wearing popular trainers, caps, clothes and the like. The average person wants to be rich, famous and successful, but because they do not make it, they at least want to wear what they believe such people wear and thereby identify with them. It makes them feel good to think "Wow, now I am wearing a Nike baseball cap, the type Rap DJ, the famous rapper, was wearing in the magazine. I cannot be doing that badly." The truth is that they are really doing badly because they are spending a lot of money buying things in order to look like somebody who was paid a lot of money to wear those things. It is a loser's game, and they are at the bottom and losing end of things. If drawn, the scenario would look like a pyramid, with our wannabe friend at the ground level. He has the least money, but is exploited the most, because he is both naive and too blind to see, even though he has eyes.

Be convinced you really need those stuffs before dipping your hand into your pocket.

Be sure that that item you're buying is going to enrich your life, or that of someone else. Of course, paying a bit more for that better fitting shirt (instead of buying the cheapest, poorly tailored one) counts. If the more expensive one fits better and adds that extra spring to your steps, then paying more could be justified. What would not make sense is spending more just because the shirt has the label of a popular designer (who gives no toss about you), whether it is good value for the extra money spent or not. In the process of dipping your hand into your pocket lies a lot of power. Be aware of this enormous power and use it wisely. Make those who are after your money, for commercial purposes, sweat before they get it. The moment you hand that hard-earned money over to them, I want you to be aware of the fact that you don't just hand money over to them, you also hand power and freedom over to them. Do they cherish this? Do they deserve it? You have to be sure.

People have variously attempted to describe the nice feeling they have when they're spending money. One of the reasons for this is the added sense of being very powerful. At the very moment they are spending the money, they feel invincible. They can buy whatever they want and be whatever they want. There is also a sense of freedom. This is the kind of freedom that knows no boundaries. It is easy to become addicted to this feeling. Lots of people are. They derive so much pleasure from buying things that all they can think about at the intervals is the next episode of spending binge. It is like any other form of addiction.

4.8   You need more than trust

The major problem here is the tendency, which is more in some cultures than others, to believe without questioning; to believe wholeheartedly, but without reason. Some people call this to trust somebody or an establishment, but then so much so as to assume that your interest is being taken into consideration by that person you trust.

Like I said, some cultures make their people vulnerable by their very nature. In most families, you learn that you have to be obedient to be considered a good child. Everything that an older person or society and its institutions say has to be accepted as the Gospel truth. That is what you are expected to do if you come from a 'good family' and have 'good upbringing'. You do not ask questions, you do not question things, you accept whatever you're told. You try, like everybody else, not to rock the boat.

The problem is that the world has become very competitive, and will get even more competitive. What happens when things get competitive? Well, what happens in competitive situations is that the best, and only those who are able to back up their ability with going that extra mile, those who are most daring and bold, survive. It is one of the laws of nature that the strong, who are additionally very adaptive, are able to go ahead and survive. The same rule in fact applies to the whole species of living things – those unable to weather the storm get slaughtered. We as human beings are supposed to be more civilised and to be our brothers' keepers. But for your own good, my son, don't wait for that brother or you could wait forever. Worse still is that the wait could still end up being in vain. Don't actually expect that 'best friend' to show up, so that if he does come to your rescue it would be a bonus.

You stand absolutely no chance in the world if you constantly expect others to stand up for you and protect your best interest. That would be too much to expect. Think of it for a second, why would they? What would be the incentive? What would be in it for them? What would they stand to gain? OK, you could once in a while come across people who are generous and caring, but it would be safer not to expect to be offered more than crumbs and leftovers from them. I believe this to be the healthy way of thinking

It is maybe similar to running a race, boxing or any other form of sport for that matter. People are in it to win. Winning is both part of the game and the fun. How you carry yourself after you would have won and *become* a champion is something else, but first you have to strive to win.

You will get nowhere if you keep **expecting** other people to help you. It is not part of the game. If someone offers to assist you along the way, think about it first. Do you really want this person's help? What are the terms and conditions? – find out. Why are they doing it and what do they want in return? – think about it. You do not have to be unnecessarily suspicious, but you always need to know where you stand and what the motive is. The best and easiest way to get things done is by working in, and as part of, a group or a team. For such a team to succeed, however, it would have to depend on the efforts of the individual members. This is the difference between team sports like football and other sports activities like tennis. In a team, everybody must put in their best before success can be achieved. Team spirit has to exist. If the team goes ahead and accomplishes its goals, then everybody gains and is happy. It would neither be fair nor right, even when one is operating in a team, to **expect** the same level of support. It is a bonus if one does. Some would see this as a disadvantage in team sports. Remember that a team can only function smoothly, and the team members put in their best, if they all have the same aims, level of motivation and objectives, and if they have the same interests at heart. It would be a case of trying to get something for nothing where above is not the case, in which circumstance, one is bound to fail. Be wary of expecting something from others, and even more so when you have not made any contribution. So always ask yourself, what have I brought to the table?

4.9 Smokescreens

It is OK to be able to trust other people. It is in fact a necessity, but let them gain this trust first. Until then, be nice, fair, non-judgemental and open-minded, but not a lot more in your first encounter with others. That way what you're doing is only an attempt to protect yourself. Nobody else is expected to do this for you. Attempt should additionally be made to consciously make the effort not to judge too quickly, hence to avoid rushing to a conclusion about others.

Opening up completely to a total stranger, on the other hand, has nothing to do with trust, but everything to do with stupidity. Even by definition, trust grows, and is developed with time. Trust has to do with lowering your defences. You only lower your defences if you have the feeling that you are safe, that you are not vulnerable and that you will not be taken advantage of.

You have not seen a live tortoise as yet, but you are very familiar with snails which are seen at the back of our house in summer. You have always shown a fascination for them. Both are strange-looking, but interesting animals. They are also different from each other, but one thing they have in common is that neither the tortoise nor the snail would stick its head out of its shell unless it was convinced there was no impending harm or danger. It might sound old-fashioned, and maybe a bit boring, but it works for them. It is a lesson probably worth acknowledging, taking into account that the tortoise is one of the animals that lives the longest.

This is certainly another case of trying to find a good balance – especially since it would on the other hand not be correct to appear 'cold' in your first meetings. The opposite should actually be the case. Endeavour to be warm, friendly, bright, open and helpful, but at the same time be quick to know where the boundary is in the early stages of your meeting with people.

You should, as mentioned, accordingly be slow to jump to conclusion about others. Remain open-minded, neutral and give them a chance before reaching conclusions about them.

You want to avoid making the mistake that former leaders of some African countries made in the past. Many of them signed away the resources and the future of next generations to foreign businessmen and governments, mostly out of naivety and sometimes out of greediness and narrow-mindedness. Some of them were just too trusting and too slow to realise or accept the possibility of ulterior motives. What would also have worked against some of them was the belief that the visitors were so well off that they possibly could not have wanted anything tangible from the indigenes. This approach continues to work very well. The person likely to succeed in being granted favour, including financial, is the person who is able to somehow come across as not being desperate, the one able to conceal the dire state of their circumstance so well that they easily pass as lacking a need. They almost get away with the impression they're doing their potential victim a favour. Do not underestimate the importance of external impression and smokescreens.

4.10   You have no right

It is similar, on the other hand, to people who think they have the right to certain privileges. This could be very annoying for the person at the giving end. You will certainly come across such people, who are convinced that being your relation or being connected to you in one way or the other gives them certain rights over you, your possessions or your time. So strong is their conviction often that they then develop a sense of entitlement that not even you have over your belongings, for you at least have some element of gratitude and appreciation, especially when you remember what you went through to acquire the item in question. I am talking of people who would want to take your things, convinced that you are obliged to hand them over and that it is within their right to simply take.

Even when you think you have a certain right to take other people's possessions, no matter what they are, try your best to at least take what they are with some respect. And when you have received what it is you're after, show some appreciation. It sounds simple and understandable, but certainly not for people who believe, wrongly, that you are obliged to do what you did.

Be aware of this character, but don't copy it.

It is different when you have worked for, and contributed towards something, in which case you're taking what belongs to you.

4.11   Don't get rich quick

I read somewhere that 80% of the people who won the lottery would have lost all their money after five years or would be worse off. I personally think the figures to be a little bit exaggerated, but could also see how it could be true.

Making and keeping money is more of a science than an art. This means that it follows a certain formula which can be reproduced over and over again and would work for anybody, or at least almost anybody. It also means that it obeys certain laws.

The sure way to know how to handle money is therefore to learn the ways of money. There are no two ways. It is one of those things you learn by doing, and in which you become better with time and with practice. The trick is to figure out what needs to be done, then stick to it and repeat the process, amidst hiccups, which are almost expected to occur along the way.

The most difficult, but certainly also the best part of the process is the learning. It is in the learning that characters become modified, eyes become opened and are able to see things that untrained eyes do not see. The best part is that the learning becomes the asset. It is the most important bit. Once learned, you can have it all your life as long as you do not forget to regularly refresh the knowledge by always trying to keep up to date. The road, the journey itself, is the most difficult, yet the most rewarding. There are hardly shortcuts; you either learn and know it or you don't. If you know the rule, you can always apply it. So that even if you're unfortunate enough to miss your step and fall, all you need do is to apply the same rules and you would again be on your way to riches. Learn therefore to cherish the journey itself and maintain your level of motivation by constantly reminding yourself of the reward that awaits you.

So, what do you think would happen to the person who comes into possession of large sums of money without first learning the rules? They simply would not stand a chance against the inevitable. It would be like trying to run without first putting in the time to learn how to stand, and then to walk before progressing to running. It would be a predictable disaster that can't wait to happen.

You will also come across the same problem when people are left the sort of money they're not used to, say by a rich relative. It is usually not much different to what happens to the children of very rich parents. The other set of people that tend to suffer as much as lottery winners though are very successful sports stars and musicians, usually from troubled families. Sudden accumulation of wealth tends to simply mess up their heads. Being surrounded by slugs and leeches, in the form of yes men, does certainly not help. The fall is usually very disastrous and painful, even to watch, despite it being predictable. The common denominator with all these people is the absence of the necessary skills needed to manoeuvre the double-edged sword called money. It is a skill that is poorly transferable or heritable (otherwise children of very rich parents will have it in abundance, and they usually don't). It instead has to be learned and, as is with all skills, gets better with use.

You will come across a lot of people promising you ways of becoming very rich very quickly. This will very often be for a fee. Avoid such people as much as you can. Do not be tempted. If what they promise to sell could be so easily bought, they would very much keep it to themselves or sell it to people they know. Do not confuse them with people offering genuine services. A major difference is that the person who has something genuine to offer should be, and would also sound, less enthusiastic. They will also put you under less pressure to hand over your money. If you, however, generally speaking, trust your instinct and do not get greedy, you will almost always know when to ignore the promise of some people to bring you heaven on Earth. The whole thing would sound over-salted, too good to be true.

The only person assured of quick money from such an encounter is the very person promising to make you rich. You only need to visit a casino and keep a watchful eye to see what I mean. The only person **guaranteed** to get rich is the owner of the casino. He is the one in business.

But even then, of what use is the money to the person who obtains it quickly before he knows how to handle it? He could as well have willingly taken his time to learn and to feel the joy of overcoming the obstacles he would face along the way. This is where the fun is.

4.12 There are lots of things to worry about, girls are not one of them

Lots of people associate girls and women with wasting time and money, hence my decision to touch on people of the opposite sex here. One of the best things that will happen in your life is an association with a good woman. One of the worst things that could happen to you is a bad woman crossing your path. It could be that extreme. You have to be ripe and ready. The ripeness meant has little to do with age.

Because women can have a strong influence on your life, and because they always will be there, I would want to suggest that girls can wait. You have to be ready first. Do not be afraid to explore, to experiment, again to have fun if you can handle it, and as long as nobody is hurt.

I am yet to hear of a man who became great because he allowed his dreams, goals and aspirations to become smothered by the influence of a woman, to the detriment of those goals. Stories, however, abound about men who have allowed women to ruin them. The bottom line, and in order to spell it out, because of the level of importance of this topic, my son, is – don't lose your head.

Don't get me wrong here though. I am not saying, my son, be cold. Of course not. Some will say of me, but he lost his head and married a woman of different tradition, culture and colour; should he not have married one like himself? So, did he lose his head or not? I do not have to justify my actions, and here would be the wrong medium for a clarification of that issue anyway. But it goes to strengthen my point, that at the right point, when you are ready, you will be more able to stand firm because you have what it takes to make a relationship with a woman work. You will at this point also be able to handle the challenges and the criticism that would result from a relationship. But rush into women without your head, and you could end up completely losing it.

I don't know for sure but the musician called Jay-Z could be alluding to this same point when he wrote (and sang) '99 Problems', in which he was, as far as I could understand it, stating that he had so many problems as a young Black man but the problems due to a girl would not be enough to be counted as one of them. For a long time in your life, despite the sorrow and the pain you could temporarily face, I would say that you ensure the same applies to you. Very few women will be worth the extra effort, and that is a good thing.

4.13   Pray

There is something very powerful about a clear sense of purpose, direction and aim. It is even more effective if such desire can be expressed in clear words, or even better, written down. The icing on the cake is the ability to write such desire so clearly that the date by when it should become reality is also indicated.

Now comes the even more crucial point. Something dramatic happens when you have full faith in what you so strongly desire surely happening. Your faith has to be so strong that you can see (with your eyes closed) and almost experience that which you desire. You are therefore effectively not just wishing your heart's desire would happen, you *know* it will happen and you can in fact already feel it, because your belief is that strong.

If prayer, as it is unfortunately not the case with a lot of people, is the means of being able to have such strong faith and belief that what you so intensely desire will come true, then one could ask why not pray? Why not pray, as long as what is being done goes beyond a senseless and mechanical recitation of some meaningless religious dogma that would not have any positive impact on your life, those around you or the world at large?

The bottom line and the challenge, on the other hand, would be that of discovering a method that works best for you, to achieve the same goal of having absolute faith in your specific heart's desire coming true.

The need to believe so strongly in the desired outcome that it can be perceived through the senses is so important that I'm emphasising it again. Prayer helps some people achieve this by the same desire being repeated on a regular basis (say twice a day). One gradually gets to the point where one has full faith in the particular desire turning to reality.

The next thing prayer could do is to help the person reciting the prayer to keep this strong desire constantly in their mind. What most people don't realise is that their minds are very rarely blank. There is always something on one's mind, whether one wants it or not. Most people also do not realise by how much that which we constantly have on our mind shapes our lives, and even more importantly, becomes a reality. The chances of this reality occurring are additionally dependent on how much we desire such thoughts. Linking this desire with faith is normally the final piece of the puzzle.

If prayer helps you to achieve your heart's desires and to be a better person, then, my son, by all means pray. Pray then not merely once a day, but say short prayers several times a day. Just ensure the content of your prayer is clear, focused, concise, to the point and that it is mixed with faith. Be sure you're not just making a wish, as most people do, but that you are instead communicating what you *know* deeply in your heart is sure to happen. There are few things more powerful than this.

5

Love

5.1 Candles

A burning candle will get used up anyway. Where it is placed is immaterial. It will get used up anyway.

Think for a moment of us humans as candles. We gained light when we were born; we're going to lose it when we die. They are not quite comparable, but let's, for the purpose of illustration, see death as the point the light gets extinguished.

Now think about a cellar, how dark, wet and cold it could be. Then a table in the cellar. The cellar is empty, except for a few rats and cockroaches.

Now imagine a burning candle, placed under the table in the cellar.

Compare the above candle with another, similar one. This one is exactly the same as the first one. The only difference is in the location, for this second candle has been lit and placed **on** a table in the open space at night. The location is the back of the house. And it is a nice and warm summer night. The members of a family are sitting around the candle. They have just had dinner and are now sitting around, relaxing, recounting how their day went. There is no other source of light apart from the one from the candle. The light from the candle is so strong it attracts even insects, which flock to it. This candle has almost a central position in the gathering.

The two candles will both burn out with time. So much is clear and uniform. Both are doing great jobs of illuminating their surroundings to the best of their abilities.

The candle hidden under the table in a cellar, though doing the best it can, under the circumstances, could be said to be wasting away. It has a very strong and potentially useful tool – the flame, but this is of no use to anyone. The saddest part, I think, is that this candle could have been of much use and it would have cost it absolutely nothing extra. It would also not have to put in extra effort, possibly except ensuring it is not extinguished by the wind, in order to be of more use.

It is, generally speaking, easier to be nice to others, to be of use to the people around us. It usually does not cost us a lot, if anything at all, extra.

Being nice and showing love comes in different shapes and forms, depending (where applicable) on the existing relationship. There, however, does not need to be a relationship before one should be nice.

Start with the simplest things – be happy and let it manifest through a smile on your face. A smile is often considered simple, but is so powerful – it can very quickly influence the people you meet, who would then be very likely to reciprocate with the same attitude, and the people they meet to do the same, and so on, thereby setting up a kind of chain reaction. All at no cost to you.

5.2   Show love

Always go out of your way and put in that extra effort in order to be of use to others. It is so uplifting, the thought that you've been useful and contributory to somebody else's well-being.

Problem is that we live in a world where it is not cool to be nice. Being nice, polite and helpful is thought of as being qualities for people who are weak; for people who cannot protect or look after themselves. The message or impression that one tends to get is to question why someone who is self-assured and who exudes enough self-confidence would need to be nice to others. Being nice is therefore seen as reserved for people who need favours; for 'softies'. The general attitude is that strong, self-reliant and very independent people do not necessarily need to be nice. They can 'afford' not to be nice to others.

Everything has become very fast paced, so that people are generally rushing to catch up. You will be expected to rush around. You will also be expected to be aggressive in your dealings, and it will be understandable that you have to do that in order to survive. The person who does not comply is seen as having a problem, apart from being weak and not having the courage and bravado to appear and to act mean.

It is true, and there is no disputing that a lot of people have a lot of stress, just as you probably will as well. I will, however, ask you not to allow the pressure to be an excuse.

There are many parts of the world where people look at you very strangely if you laugh out loud in public. They fail to see, or even imagine, what could be so funny.

Learn to show love, my son. Be of help to those who you come across. There is a lot of joy in doing that.

It is moreover more gratifying and satisfying to give than to receive. It might not fit into many of the things you have learnt, but it is very true that the more you give, the more you will receive. Even from an economic point of view, the more people your actions impact on, the more successful you're likely to be.

5.3   You never know

Even if seen from a selfish point of view, it is said that it is good to be good to the person you meet on your way up, since you do not know who you will meet on your way down. The only thing that is constant and which remains the same is change itself. It is well to ignore or even refuse the fact, once things are moving on fine for us, that we will ever require another person's help. What folly. What utter nonsense. It is similar to a nation, at its peak, believing that it will remain the world super power for ever. The leaders of such a country would not need to go far in the history books to be reminded that nations, and sometimes continents, usually have periods of rise, which are then followed by periods of fall. So that you have the rise and fall of the Ethiopian Empire; the rise and fall of the Egyptian Empire; the rise and fall of the Roman Empire and the rise and fall of the Chinese Empire, just to give you an idea. At their peak, these nations were the most powerful and often most feared in the world. Today most of them are a mere shadow of themselves. So fewer things could be better predictable. Such cycles are bound to take place, it often is just a question of how long the time intervals would be. The fall of individuals after periods of great achievement is less predictable, but always remains a possibility.

Years of hard work can, in some instances, culminate in it taking seconds for the shift from a condition of abject want and need to that of riches to take place. The loss of wealth could even be much faster and more dramatic. There are, therefore, often no guarantees. Past records and the present state of things with a person do, therefore, **not** give a clue as to how the future of that person would turn out to be. Virtually everything is possible. It is true that the chances of such drastic change taking place is higher in a person who is generally exposed to more risk, the impact of such changes is additionally also much more pronounced with such people.

So even for selfish reasons, would it then not be wise to be nice to the people you interact with daily, especially as the tables could turn so quickly?

I see no argument, whatsoever, against showing love on a daily basis to the people you come across everyday, no matter how brief the encounter.

5.4   Which love? What love?

Fewer words have been more wrongly interpreted, conveyed or understood. The word love means different things to different people, making it not the easiest word to use. There are too many meanings for the word. This has in some instances even led to a total avoidance of the word, in order not to cause any form of confusion.

To make things even more confusing though, the word love is additionally used by most people to describe feelings of great affection for something, i.e. not for human beings. The confusing bit for most people is that the same word used to qualify and convey very strong feelings for other human beings could also be used to describe feelings for a dog, for good weather, for good food and wine, and for a nice house. This multipurpose usage of the word could possibly have added to the dilution of its meaning.

Then there are those people who use the word love so freely to describe feelings for other human beings that there is no emotional attachment, no form of seriousness to the use of the word. They say the words "I love you" so often, so void of emotion, so loosely, so mechanically that the words have absolutely no meaning, and have nothing to do with the context in which they are supposed to be used. These words could become so distant and said with so much detachment that saying them would as well have meant something like "How are you?" for the user. Nothing whatsoever to do with the said words – just something to say when you don't know anything else to talk about, or to fill gaps during conversations, but nothing to be taken literally.

So, it is worth noting that the word love, especially when used to convey feelings, should always be questioned in the depth of your mind. It often is not what you think it means. The word love is even used by some to take advantage of and to manipulate others, who are not informed enough, or do not know what you now know. It is a shame, but important to be aware that love is not always as good as it sounds. Some people see the word as a master key, the one to use when everything else fails; the ace in the pack of cards to flash when it becomes critical to win the game.

Do not allow yourself to be taken advantage of in the name of love. Real love is not in any form selfish, cold, calculating, mean, egocentric and self-centred, greedy and inconsiderate. Love has nothing to do with taking advantage of situations and of somebody. Real love is the opposite of all the above, and much more.

So, when you hear this word being used, first think of the context in which it is being applied… should you become more alert or should you gently drop your guard?

5.5   Stupid love

The very good news is that real love exists though. It just gets more and more difficult to find in this time and age. Love is one of those things you can unfortunately not describe. You will just know love when you come across it. Your heart will tell. It is only your heart that knows it is love. Your head will most likely miss it, because it will want to compare, and apply logic. Love does, however, often not follow logic. It is, therefore, very difficult to attempt loving with the head and explains why people often fail to see what the person in love sees. True love comes more from the heart. It goes with the flow. It is not calculating or scheming.

Love should, however, not be confused with infatuation. Infatuation is when you think you are madly (yes, madly) in love with someone, often shortly after meeting them. The truth, however, is that you are not – you are neither mad nor in love. With time, you will see that it is easy to know the difference between the two. Infatuation, to start with, often does not last long. It is usually a short, but very intense, experience. Think of it as a storm. It can be equally as destructive as the storm if confused with love. Infatuation and love are worlds apart and have almost nothing to do with each other. One is very fast, almost furious, and often leaves unmistakeable marks of destruction along its path, while the other is calm, relaxing, peaceful, patient and tranquil.

You will often recognise infatuation when it hits you. Whether you know it is infatuation or not, just remain calm and don't do anything heroic in the very early stages of a relationship, especially if your instinct is trying to tell you something. Allow the relationship time to prove and establish itself. Is it love or is it infatuation? The amount of energy infatuation dissipates is so much that it is unsustainable at that level, so that infatuation, given time, will very quickly tire and let you be.

There are factors which must be in place for love to manifest and to be sustained. It is otherwise like a one-legged table – it is bound to fall as soon as you take your hands off it.

The love that exists between a man and a woman would best be said not to be pure, innocent love in some circles and societies. Love has a different meaning in such circles, and could even be said to be non-existent. This is because it is felt not to be 'pure' but instead only manifests (usually from the female perspective) if certain (often materialistic) criteria are met. There is a lot of debate regarding if what such people feel could really be termed love and if they could not be excused as being influenced purely by their economic status. The problem, however, is that you find such people (who profess to being in love with someone who is financially better off) in both poor and rich societies. It is just differently manifested. Within such a circle of people, love as I have tried to describe it hardly exists. The instinct to survive is much stronger than the need to feel, enjoy and express love. So, one of the first points that goes through the head of a girl (and her people) when she meets a boy, and he proposes, then becomes – is he financially stable enough to take good care of me (and maybe my family)? Finance takes centre stage. It is only after this, and similar questions, could be answered to the affirmative, that one goes to the next stage of convincing one's self that what one feels is love. This way of thinking works for the people involved in many instances, but still should not be confused with love, but more a means to an end.

It is true that a few things are often and, in fact, should be in place, and even considered, before we 'allow' ourselves to fall in love, but this process of assessing how suitable the other person is is never this judgemental or analytical. The emphasis is also usually on actually more 'trivial' things like tone of voice, manners, physical attraction, behaviour, similar ideologies, etc. The cases described (above), in comparison, are more of a war, a battle to survive against odds. Instead of the heart, the head is given priority here. A decision is first of all made here about whether to love, based purely on if financial security, or at least strong hope for that to materialise in the future, does exist. The heart is pushed to a corner and is not allowed to play a major role in this crucial decision-making process.

It is not pleasant, and neither does it give the best of feelings, to be loved, not for you, but because of what is believed you can provide. If someone crosses your path who is looking for a cash cow or a hen that lays golden eggs, be kind and direct them to the next farm and remember to wish them luck. It only makes sense that first you sow, then you talk of reaping. This has nothing to do with trying to be a provider and being generous. It has everything to do with being taken advantage of. The term 'love' being used to make this a less bitter pill to swallow cannot completely remove the bad taste it leaves in the mouth.

The tricky bit is not allowing being financially well-off to drive you to paranoia. It will be much more difficult, but you still need to, somehow, find love. Just be at least aware, and decide on how to address the issue of fair-weather love.

5.6   Love hurts

Note, however, that even true love is not just all bliss and fun. Love could be a dangerous and very risky thing. Part of the reason is that in order to be truly in love, you have to let so much go, you have to close an eye to a lot of things, you have to open up and allow yourself to be understood, you have to once in a while play the fool and you have to be ready to make compromises. All these make you very vulnerable and increase the chances of you getting hurt. The worst bit is that in order to be in love and to practise love, you have to, even though you are aware of the above, take some calculated risks, open up and take the plunge. Scary, almost. But that is the nature of love, and the fun of it. You know you could be hurt, but you do not allow the fear of that to have the upper hand. So as is with most scary things that need to be done, you still go ahead and do it anyway while you brace yourself for the consequences. One cannot talk of love if there is no element of exposure and sharing. It is not love if only the head is used all the time. It can only be termed love if the heart and gut feeling are sometimes deliberately allowed to be in charge, despite the head screaming itself coarse while trying to remind anybody who would listen of the potential risk of falling flat on your face.

When you have found love, next thing is to have the courage to go for it and hold on to it. You could get criticised and misunderstood. Do not blame the people who do, they just don't see what you see, nor do they feel what you feel. Love is, however, 95% feeling and does not tend to comply to mathematical formulae, so how would they know?

5.7   Feel love

You would have seen that it takes some element of selflessness and kindness and sometimes a lot of foolishness, yet courage to give, to appreciate and to feel love.

This should, however, not deter you.

Love, being a universal phenomenon, is the same, is communicated in the same language and follows the same basic principles the world through.

Love is like a nutrient, a nutrient for the mind and the soul. He who tries to live without love, though not a physical death, dies.

I'd rather die physically than to die spiritually.

Keep your head, my son, but let go when you can, and when the time is right, feel love.

6

Don't forget money

6.1   The origin

Money. Money is a complicated one. Of all the things we have discussed so far, this is certainly one of the most difficult topics to talk about. The idea behind its discovery is quite simple – to make transactions and exchange of goods and services easy. Before the introduction of money, people practised what was known as trade by barter. This effectively meant that what someone had was exchanged for something else, that somebody else wanted. If you wanted, for instance, a bicycle, you had to find somebody who was selling a bicycle and give the person what he or she would accept in exchange for their bicycle. This might sound as if it would have been fun, but it sure wasn't. It was actually as complicated as it sounds, for first you had to find the person selling something, then you had to pray you had something they wanted. The two of you then had to work out a value for the quantity of what you want to exchange for the bicycles (in your example) that the person would accept as being truly equivalent to their bicycle.

It was realised that an acceptable, common, reproducible form of exchange was needed. Different forms of articles and objects were tried, and discarded until the intelligent idea of money evolved.

6.2   Forms of money

Although there are more complicated forms of financial exchange, let's, for simplicity, reduce forms of money to just two – coins and paper. Yes, paper money is made from paper. Paper is produced from trees. It is true that notes indirectly come from trees, but very wrong to say or even think that money grows on trees. I know there are people who are convinced otherwise, but please listen to such a way of thinking as you would to a fairy tale. It should go in through one ear, and come out of the other. Also keep in mind the fact that the people who think of money as growing on trees are usually not the ones making the money.

There are also no machines that freely spit out money. Well, there are, but they mainly spit out your own money. So what these machines give me when we go to collect money at the cash machine is not free money. It is my money; our money. The machine only gives out money if somebody has money in the bank. If I do not have any money in the bank, but still try to withdraw money at a cash machine I will be given nothing. There are ways of borrowing money that is not yours from such machines, but I will advise you to leave this for now.

I remember the look on your face when you saw and realised that people could pay for goods in shops without giving out money. You only saw them scribble something, and they were then handed the things they wanted. It all looked so cool. I am not sure if you would change your opinion if I were to tell you that the money those people were spending, in the majority of such cases, was not even theirs. They were mostly spending borrowed money. Buying with borrowed money normally costs more because interest would have to be paid. It could also have been their money that they were spending. It was either their money, in which case there is no interest, or it was not their money, in which case things could become more expensive if they have to pay interest. There is, however, nothing like free money – no matter how the money is being spent.

6.3   The ways people see money

Money and people's attitude to it are difficult to explain, so I will understand if you get confused there. You, however, still have to pay extra attention here.

Many people do not know what stance to take when it comes to money. Many think it better still to ignore money-related issues altogether. You know, like the ostrich that hides by sticking its head into the sand.

Money has been described by some as the root of all evil. Some others, on the other hand, have the other extreme view about money and say that money makes the world go round. Many others still simply do not have any opinion about money. For them money exists, but does not merit talking about – there are more important things to talk about, they argue. Or money is seen as being so dirty and disgusting, they just cannot get themselves to talk about it. This is not helped by the fact that money is seen by a lot of people as taboo. It should just not be mentioned. One of the most uncomfortable things to talk about, by such people, is income – how much they earn. No, they will not talk about that but will instead spend a lot of their free time reading tabloid papers that contain gossip about what celebrities earn.

6.4   How do you see money?

I know you are intelligent, so will be able to come to your own conclusion later. For that is what we as human beings have to do. We do whatever we do and have certain opinions based on what we are convinced is the situation of things. People around us, our parents, our teachers, our friends, the mass media and society as a whole can only supply us with information and ideas. They will all try to influence us into behaving the way they think is right and appropriate. The direction we decide to go is, however, ultimately our, and no other person's, decision.

How you see, define and handle money is therefore your decision, which is good, although I remain curious to know which way you go.

6.5   0 (Zero) and X people

You have two extreme cases:
- The set of people who fail or do not want to realise the above points, for whatever reason. Let's call them the zero people, and remember them with 0.
- Then you have those who are very much aware, in fact too aware, of the previously made points. Let's call them the extreme people, and remember them with X.

The viewpoint of X people

X people could be individuals, societies or governments. These people know so much about the power of money that it influences most of their decision making. Hardly anything is done without considering the financial implication. For them, nothing goes for nothing. They believe so very strongly in money that one could describe them as worshipping money. They believe that anything, and anybody, can be bought, one just needs to find the price.

Zero people and money

0 people do not care about money. Money is such a minor issue that it is not even mentioned in conversations. This group of people is, however, always in need of one thing or the other, for which it is dependent on outsiders. Their eyes are, however, so clouded by their immediate needs that they are unable to look far enough to realise the origin of their wants. They, once in a while, become clearly aware of having a massive problem, but because they are ignorant of the origin of their problems, they make themselves believe that they are not in the position to do a lot to better their situation. They then become victims of circumstances which they are convinced they cannot change. They always have somebody to blame for their condition.

These two are opposites and are extreme cases. It is, however, good to be aware of them.

6.6   Don't ignore money

A fact that is, however, so clear and crucial that I have to emphasise it is that it would, no matter your standpoint, be a mistake to completely forget about money. Thinking about it, it seems easier to be able to list the things you do not need money for, than to try to name the things you need money for. That is how fundamental money is. The lack or absence of money may not make the world stand still, but things will come close to that. Did you know that people who cannot afford to buy something to eat can simply die of hunger? I know it could sound like a story from one of your comic books, but believe me when I tell you that a lot of people starve to death because they do not have enough to eat. To die of starvation must be a sad and terrible way to die.

A twist in the suggestion not to forget money is that you would have less stress in life, be happier and, ultimately, have a higher chance of making a lot of money if you do something not primarily because of the money, but because you like and enjoy what you do. Doing what you like and enjoy doing is a recipe for comfortably making a lot of money. The best part is that if you like what you're doing that much it would not feel like working to earn a living. You would then not need to force yourself to carry out the activity that generates the money, since you could even imagine doing the same thing all the time and could even do it for free. It is sad when working is associated with suffering, with unwanted stress. It is then that every Monday becomes another manic Monday – like they sang in the song.

So, don't ignore money but let this awareness be somewhere at the very back of your mind. Avoid the temptation, if you can, of choosing a vocation just for the money. You could otherwise, at some point, feel as if you are selling your soul, or exchanging a part of you for the money and even if you eventually have the money a large hole could still be possibly felt deep in you somewhere.

A key point, once again, is that we are here talking about the journey called life and we know that in life anything goes – you can live to be 100 years and you could die tomorrow, so why not do what you enjoy doing anyway? You could decide that you would 'do what you have to do' and make the money first, and then plan your life, which of course is a good possibility. The point, however, is that in life there are no guarantees. How do you know you will ever make money, how do you know how long the process will take, how do you know you will live to enjoy the fruits of your labour, or that you will get to the end of the journey in one piece? How do you know? The truth of course is that no one knows, and that is not a bad thing.

6.7   Is money bad?

Money in itself cannot be the root of all evil, as some people claim. It is a material thing. It is not even a living thing, since it has no life of its own. In this modern world, where most transactions do not involve physical cash, one can even question if money is real. This is, however, irrelevant. What I want you to realise is that what matters is what you do with money. It is basically like anything else in life – a knife, education, knowledge, freedom, a relationship, your time. Ultimately what matters when in possession of any of these things is what you decide, or believe, you can do with them. You are in charge. You determine what happens. It is your choice.

You can for instance cut vegetables with a knife. You will, however, cut your finger by mistake if you're not careful. Another person can also decide to knowingly cause harm with the same knife. So would they say that knives are, on their own, evil? Of course not. It all has to do with the person handling the knife. The same applies to money. Money in itself is actually not the important thing. It is what you do with it and the meaning you attach to it that counts. You can save lives with money, but then people also get killed for, and because of, money all the time.

There is a story of a man who had a good life. He was generally well liked in the community, especially by his wife, his kids and his friends. He was a nice, honest man. One day he was told that he had won the lottery. He played during a fundraising event and did not take his chances of winning seriously. He won a very large sum of money. Suddenly he found out that he could buy all the things he always wanted to buy but did not have the money to. He, however, could not manage the situation because he got influenced by all the money and started drinking and treating his family badly. He did not care about anything any more.

Gradually, everybody, including members of his family, started to leave him. He became a lonely, sad man. He started to blame the money for his troubles. He one day decided he'd had enough. He went to his last remaining friend and begged him to save him by taking the money. His friend was very reluctant to take the money because he, like everybody else, knew the story of his friend and his evil money. He finally accepted to collect the money, but on one condition – nobody should know that he was now in possession of the money. The rich man thanked him and handed him all the money and immediately became a poor man again. That same night the man who now had the money went to the back of his house and dug a large hole, then he carefully wrapped all the money and put it into the hole which he covered up when he was done. He collected the money from his friend only because he pitied him and wanted to help him out. He personally wanted nothing to do with the money. Because he had seen what the money did to his friend, he told no soul a word about it. He died a poor man, with the money all the while wasting away in the hole at the back of his house. A crucial point though was that while alive, he felt much better and more at ease with being poor. This was, as far as he was concerned, easier to deal with than being in possession of all that cursed money.

The ideal scenario, in my opinion, is that those who do not have the knowledge, or the ability, to do certain things should steer clear of them and leave it to those who can. I'm for the same reason not a big fan of DIY (Do It Yourself) in the house. I'm not good at it, the finished job will almost inevitably not be as good as that done by a professional and it could potentially be dangerous. Worse still is that I often, therefore, will find it a waste of my time, especially as it will surely take me much more time than it would take someone who knows what they are doing and who has the opportunity of being an expert, even by the sheer number of times he carries out such activities. There is hardly a reason why the same cannot be said for large sums of money. Those who desire large sums of money would be best advised to work on how to use it first. It will be time worth spending. The consequence of not doing so could otherwise be tragic. It would be futile to turn round and blame money afterwards. It, except in the case of the poisoned chalice of inherited large sums of money, did not force its way into its owner's hands, but poured in at one's insistence and request.

Someone once said, I have been poor and I have been rich, and I know which one I prefer. I can also imagine which one he would prefer.

Another way to look at it, irrespective of what one thinks, even if one is convinced that one does not have a need for money, is the extent of good use money can, if properly managed, be put to. There are so many people for whom it is a case of life or death because of their level of poverty. Making life more bearable for such people, in the absence of other uses, is worth striving for.

6.8   You decide

Money does not make one happy. This is one of the phrases you will hear a lot. There are many of such. I will not try to prove which opinion is right, and which is wrong. One thing I can tell you is that money on its own will neither make you sad nor happy. It all depends on you. Poor people are not generally unhappy by default and neither are they happy all the time. What influences their state of mind are their **values**, and their priorities; what they see as being important and what they therefore focus on. This incidentally also has a very strong impact on how the rich person feels most of the time. It is a person's values that affect such things as someone deciding, for instance, to spend as much of their time travelling as is possible, even if they travel with their last savings, or to spend their free time with their family instead of using the time to pursue money. They would all of course be happy, as long as they're doing what they want to do.

If somebody, however, makes the exact same decisions but does not take the consequences of their decisions into consideration, then they are being programmed for a life of misery and sadness, for they will never be happy, with or without money.

Somebody who wants to be rich, at all costs, the consequences and the price to pay for the achievement of the goal notwithstanding, is most likely to become rich, but there are also good chances they will most likely end up sad and miserable as well. The trick is to make informed decisions and to be both aware and ready to accept the consequences of our decisions. This has absolutely nothing to do with money on its own, and applies to other human wants as well. Relevant questions should therefore always include, 'Do I really want to pay such a hefty price for my dream?' and 'Will the end result be justified, and worth the sacrifice?'.

6.9   But beware

A sudden rush of money, I must re-emphasise, is very powerful. It can be as powerful as a water wave.

Because you can do so much with it, it can also get into your head and influence you to the point of intoxication. When people have had too much alcohol, they lose control – they become dangerous and aggressive; they say things they neither want to say nor would have said normally; their mood changes – for some they become very moody, while others become euphoric and overconfident; people who have had too much alcohol often become a danger to themselves and to society. They could have blurred vision, which does not help matters. Money in sufficient amounts can do all the above to the individual who is not able to control large sums of it. The individual would easily end up the victim, the one being used, by money.

6.10   Easy money

But for you personally, I think one of the most important things, regarding money, to be aware of is the illusion of easy money. These are really dangerous times in which one would have to be very cautious. A long time ago, it used to be very difficult to borrow money, be it from private or high-street lenders. Because it was nothing to be proud of, borrowers would go in the night, cap in hand and try their best to convince a prospective lender why he or she should lend them money. The availability of guarantors, substantial collaterals, and the nature of the borrower's character were some of the factors that were seriously taken into consideration. Borrowing money was very serious business, about which books have been written and dramas staged. Needless to say, that very few had the courage to go looking for loans, which played a complimentary role in the fact that few people were considered credit worthy. It was simply not easy to obtain a loan.

Things have, however, changed, and so much so that it is almost unimaginable to think of the times when things were any different. This is compounded by the extent of the change. There has in fact been a complete turnaround of events. It is the borrowers who now need protection from the lenders. This statement is worth repeating. It is the borrowers who now need protection from the lenders. In other words, the people who borrow money are now the ones who should have measures in place to avoid overexposure and exploitation by lenders. Most people are not aware of this. So that a critical point is that most people are still not aware, and therefore do not appreciate this shift. They still see it as a privilege to be able to obtain credit and therefore spend easy money which they never worked for. One of the reasons, which I will talk more about in a while, is the belief that the lender must have done checks to be sure that the prospective borrower can pay back the money before lending – hence the sense of pride for being counted as one of the selected few.

Lending money is no more done in secret or in the dark. It is now a very big business propelled by greed. Lenders now shamelessly hawk their wares and use all sorts of marketing techniques and strategies to target their victims. They do not care about means that have to be used any more or the amount of harm they could cause, as long as there is money to be made. It is a huge industry and the aim is to get a slice of the cake.

The average person traditionally works between the times of 9am to 5pm. The few people who are at home at these times and are not working have either:

- lost their job;
- not been able to get a job;
- been made house-bound by virtue of looking after a child or a person requiring care;
- recently suffered from an illness and are recovering;
- a form of handicap or the other;
- retired;
- or are too young to work.

Most of these people have an element of vulnerability. There is hardly a half-hour that passes on local television channels, during the hours of 9am and 5pm, that a company that lends money does not advertise how they would be able to lend money to this particular group of vulnerable people, watching television. These are the people who are likely to be struggling to obtain credit because of their circumstances and poor credit history. According to such adverts, all the person need do is dial a provided **free** telephone number. No case is too simple or too difficult, the viewer is promised. Getting credit is then portrayed as one of the easiest ways of getting hold of some quick money, with which one can then do whatever one wants to do.

One feels concerned for such people who have that level of vulnerability and at the same time get bombarded with such messages on a daily basis. The greater concern is, however, for the children who get exposed to such messages. The fear is that they could grow up with the belief that it is OK and acceptable, if not in fact modern and fashionable, to resort to credit, and hence easy money, in order to finance all their dreams when they grow up. It is a very dangerous trend to set and it will surely seriously affect future generations if nothing is done.

6.11 Borrowed money card

I am sure it is not only to the members of our family that credit card companies send documents asking them to complete, sign and return the form to automatically be issued credit cards, no questions asked. They promise to issue the cards, the circumstances of the person not withstanding. They normally quote mouth-watering rates, but then specify in very small print, to the few who bother to look, that obtainable rates vary and depend on the applicant's circumstances. The situation is often too tempting for the majority of the people to ignore. Worse still, they temporarily forget that what is being talked about here is BORROWED money. It would, based on the above, not be a bad idea to rename credit cards. I would vote for a credit card being called names like 'borrowed money card', or 'debt card' if a debate should arise. Such names would better define and describe what these cards really are.

Many banks use a similar technique, but in a subtler way; maybe because they often target people who have higher levels of awareness, so that when banks want to lure their 'good customers' into debt, what they do is to send letters to such people, telling them that since they are such wonderful customers, a certain amount of money, that wonderful holiday, etc., can instantly be theirs if they would only sign and return the enclosed document. The promised amount of money would then instantly become theirs, they are promised.

People should be reminded that what they are accumulating are debts, and that the money must be paid back sooner or later. If the money is not paid back as and when expected, the person's credit worthiness could be severely damaged, and this often for many years. This is actually very serious and not something that should happen to anybody, especially not to a young person whose life has barely started. It should be viewed as getting cursed.

It should be emphasised, in case it is still not clear, that people offering you such lines of credit do not do so necessarily because they like you and have your interests at heart, or because they think you have been very good and hence deserve the credit, or even worse still, because they are generous and *want to help out*. No, the only reason the banks do it is because they are the ones looking for easy money and the people being targeted are seen as the potential source of such money. It is difficult to understand, I know, but the rich plan to remain rich and get even richer and often don't care less about who is being fleeced as a result.

6.12   Learn to handle money

It is frightening that people are not prepared on how to deal with money issues. Almost stranger is how the principle of money management does not qualify to be included as part of school curricula. So much fuss is made about people getting a driving licence before they're allowed to drive. The dangers here are very apparent, mainly because the damage that could be done by somebody driving without a driving licence is physical. Human beings pay a lot of attention to physical things. These are the ones they see, so they are the issues that matter most. What they cannot see can't be that important. The truth is, however, that the reality is the other way round. I'd rather have physical than non-physical injury any day. You can see, and hence know what you're dealing with.

It is odd that lessons about how to handle money are apparently not deemed to be of the same or more importance. There is even awareness and effort gradually directed at sex education at schools. While this is a step in the right direction, one can't help but eagerly await when such education will be extended to money matters.

It is very important to educate yourself about money. Money is maybe not like a wave after all. You can tame money and that is a major difference. You can become a master over money. In which case, it becomes your servant and does exactly what you want it to do, and nothing more. That's the position to be in.

Learn as much about money as you can. Have an interest in it. Even if it is boring, even if people would rather spend it than talk about it, even if they tell you you're not supposed to and that it is not gentlemanly or polite to show an interest in money, do not listen to them, do not ignore money. Ignoring money will not make the problems you very easily could have solved with money go away.

A lot of people will want to see you as being greedy and materialistic if you show interest in learning about money and its management. Do not worry about them. Worry about yourself. Let them do so if they so please, but do not be the one who will have to go round, cap in hand, begging for money. There is little dignity in that, exccept done for the purposes of an investment, which will yield money, with which the debt is intended to be paid off.

6.13   The buck stops with you

Do also not expect ANYBODY to take care of your money for you. Even if you assign the management of the money to a professional, it still remains your responsibility. It is your responsibility to watch over your money – so accept it. You shouldn't even think of exonerating yourself from this task, just as you would not expect a fox to look after a chicken. It is not in the fox's nature to carry out such a service, and so it would not be able to. Insisting otherwise would mean asking for too much, and one should accordingly take part in accepting responsibility for whatever result that becomes obtainable. I cannot help but still feel an element of pity each time I hear stories (usually, and I wonder why) about a very rich sports person or musician blaming their accountant or financial advisers for misappropriating their money, after they've lost most of it. Somebody did apparently not explain to them that the person who will lose everything and possibly end up in jail is unlikely to be their financial adviser. Blindly handing over such enormous responsibility to someone else has to go beyond trust. It needs to extend to naivety, existing at the borders of stupidity.

Make it a point of duty to continuously educate yourself about money and how to look after it. Do not, as most people generally are, be ashamed of that. You should instead actually be proud of yourself for taking such steps and making the effort. Because what you would be doing is accepting the fact that you are responsible and that you see it as your duty to accept the responsibility.

When you follow this advice, you will initially have the feeling that money is not that easy to understand but with time you will realise that its ways follow some specific rules which can be mastered if one consistently follows the path of continuous self-development.

You will also understand that there are different categories of debt – that there is another classification of debt into 'good debt and bad debt', depending on what the borrower does with the borrowed money.

7

The butterfly effect

7.1 Catch 'em young

A common mistake is to wait and plan solely towards making it 'big'. A lot of people are like that. Gradually building, after laying good foundations, is often seen as a boring waste of time; a road that leads to nowhere, therefore only for 'losers'.

The truth, however, is that the big break will usually come, if one takes care of the slow, and seemingly less exciting and laborious, but *steady* route of gradually building up momentum. This is also the fundamental reason I want you to have access to these notes as early in your life as possible. I had my own preparation as a child. It was different, more a baptism of fire, largely from the school of hard knocks.

One of the most important lessons I've learnt is that it is ironically those small steps we take, those little, daily decisions that initially could seem almost insignificant, that then ultimately make or break us. It is those apparently insignificant choices we make that then ultimately determine where we end up. It is they, if followed up and acted upon consistently enough, that could then metamorphose into 'overnight success', for that's what observers and bystanders will see. Most people who would later adoringly comment on the success of the once child prodigy can only report things from a distance. They have little clue about the enormity of sacrifices (seemingly little sacrifices) and the price the child had to pay. They could only slightly imagine the extra bit of time spent practising, perfecting and rehearsing, most importantly, *consistently*.

Most people unfortunately are primarily interested in the loot, the final reward. They only see the final phase of the marathon that those portrayed as child geniuses have run and want to jump in, there and then, and 'compete'.

7.2   Argungu Fishing Festival

You sometimes hear scandals of people lying in wait as bystanders and then sneaking into a marathon race towards the end in their bid to reap massively but without doing what it takes. There was similarly a scandal at the Argungu Fishing Festival some years back. The festival is a very historical event that has taken place in northern Nigeria since the 1930s. It is a four-day event that ends with a fishing competition at which the person who catches the largest fish wins.

Some years back one of the contestants who was initially reported to have won the competition was shortly afterwards stripped of the title (and the opportunity to win large sums of money and gifts) and then thrown into prison after it emerged that the fish he 'caught' was dead before he brought it out of the water. The conclusion was later that he must have introduced the fish into the water before the competition. He wanted the glory, the adoration and everything else that goes with winning, but did not want to put in the hard, painful work.

Most people are like that. They want a trim body image, but do not want to forgo sweets and fatty food and neither do they want to engage in small, but regular exercise to keep fit, which would have been less stressful if done on a small but regular scale, *consistently*.

They would instead aim to 'hit the gym' at some point, while they indulge in uncontrolled food consumption and lack any form of regular exercise.

The problem with aiming to suddenly strike it big, out of nowhere, is the amount of effort (and sometimes pure luck) that is required. Putting in that level of effort, consistently, is usually not sustainable and it does not take long for the person to give up, assuming they muster the energy and courage to start in the first place. The amount of energy and commitment required to tackle the task ahead normally seem too overwhelming, to the extent that often nothing happens and procrastination sets in.

Things could (and hopefully) have changed over the years, but it took somewhere between six and twelve years to finish medical school in Vienna, Austria some years back; that was if you finished at all. The reality was that more than half of the people who started medical school dropped out. What had happened was the idea the government had to intentionally bring about a change to the social system, so that not only children from privileged backgrounds had access to university education. So not only was university education made free and students provided with all sorts of incentives (including subsidised cost of travelling and insurance) but they sometimes also received financial support. There was also (except one was a foreigner) no form of direct and specific test to determine who was offered admission for any course of study, unlike what was obtained in almost every other country. What this meant was that universities were flooded with young people, some of whom were simply shying away from their basic responsibilities and expectations, by all claiming to be studying one thing or the other. There was expectedly a lot of attraction to medicine. You can therefore imagine the sort of response I received when I, shortly after arriving in Austria, declared I was going to be studying medicine. Oh dear! What a joke! People laughed to my face and not just at the beginning. The thing is that I could understand some of the concerns expressed by some people who, even though they did not know the peculiar problem I just mentioned, were familiar with the challenges that would be associated with studying such a long, very demanding and difficult course in a foreign country, in a different language, and without much in the form of support. My parents had no idea what I was up to, let alone being in the position to provide any form of advice. The only form of communication at the time was by letters. It took several weeks (or a few months) for them to receive my letters and about the same time for me to receive theirs, if they managed to write. Financial support was something completely different – I was the one sending them money, so just don't go there.

So, you can imagine the reaction and the level of scepticism openly expressed by those around when I continued to say I was studying a few years down the line. It was tough to overlook the noise, believe in myself and keep going.

The remarkable thing, and the main point I aim to make here, is how things changed years down the line. Most of those of my countrymen who were looking for quick routes to wealth had either been deported, locked up or simply not amounted to much. Many of the other ones who saw working in factories, or in other forms of manual labour-driven jobs, as more than a means of temporarily making ends meet, have all these years remained stuck in the same rut and have still not succeeded in winning the lottery, despite all their efforts.

Nothing beats having a sense of direction than keeping focused and going slow, but *steady*. The task at hand quickly becomes a habit, a part of you and is with time executed, at least in the opinion of an observer, apparently effortlessly.

7.3   Focus

There is something about setting a goal and putting so much focus and effort into it that it takes over your being and dominates your thought process. The impact of this is magnified the clearer the goal is; the more vividly, in such a case, you can mentally picture the task at hand. The fascinating thing is that, depending on how clearly you can picture what your heart desires and how often you can remind yourself of the goal at hand, all sorts of things step in and fall in place to help ensure those dreams come true.

I know you derive pleasure in admiring the beauty of wonderfully designed sports cars. You sometimes spend time trawling the Internet in search of such vehicles and often put together what you call a PowerPoint presentation of such vehicles. You talk and think about them a lot. One of the implications of this is that you are usually the first to spot such cars when we are out and about.

> You: "Daddy, did you just see that Lamborghini?"
> Me: "Where?"
> You: "We just passed it. It was such a beauty in an unusual colour of white. I don't know if I like them in white."

> You: "Daddy, yesterday I saw a new model Ferrari. It was in black. You should have seen it."
> Me: "Wow, really? Bet it must have looked very nice."
> You: "Daddy, it was awesome."

Now these were by no means the only cars on the road. In fact, it is normally the opposite. Such vehicles are rare to come by and most people would not even see them, recognise or acknowledge them. For such people they are just cars, that maybe look 'odd and different' and also certainly not practical. So, such people could either not see them at all or 'see' them but without them registering.

This is what focus and sense of purpose could do. The reality is that our senses are constantly bombarded with loads of information at any particular point in time. The only way the body can cope is therefore to screen this information as much as possible and only allow the most important, the most pressing and the clearest impulses to register and impact on us, thereby effecting a reaction from us, both consciously and unconsciously.

Focus can also be taken to a completely different level. The particular approach depends on belief and background, but the expectation and impact differ marginally. While some people rely on incantations, others would depend on meditations, while some others would prefer to rely on various forms of prayers. All of these, other than for seeking to tap into some external forces, also more or less concentrate and narrow down the focus to the particular matter at hand. Remember what I said about all the stimuli our bodies experience, all seeking to draw away our attention. The aim, therefore, is to shut out distraction from other sources, to reduce (or aim to eliminate) the noise and instead channel our energy and the whole of our being into executing what it is we think should have priority. With time, practice and dedication, one gets better and better at it.

An important point is that we are the master of our thoughts, including our wishes and our desires. Our body and forces around us do not have a choice but to act in whatever way we decide they should. It is not for them to tell us if what we wish for ourselves is right or wrong, if it is potentially harmful (both to ourselves and others) or not or if we should actually go ahead. That aspect is our decision. So even though we have this wonderful facility at our disposal, we are solely (and nobody else is) responsible for what we decide to do with it. What happens is that the same law of nature applies to both good and bad intentions and we would achieve more or less the same goal (of our dreams coming true).

Think about the fact that a thief, in some cultures, before embarking on a 'mission' could carry out all I've told you about, to ensure he succeeds. He could carry out incantations, fast and pray and meditate, all of which could work in his favour and ensure he is successful. Some would even seek the blessing of a traditional healer, who could provide them with charms and amulets, with promises they will not be caught. Natural laws do not tend to discriminate, but rely on us to make the right choices. Their job is to obey our command, carry out our heart's desires and help us execute them.

7.4   The power of compounding

There are few forces greater than that the impact compounding would potentially have. It is based on this that you need to make haste, despite your age, and start whatever you decide it is you want to achieve as early as possible. Start small and keep going at it. You will be surprised at the momentum you would gain shortly, and remember to smile secretly to yourself when people start to comment on how lucky you have been and how you have not had to work hard at all. What do they know, or what do you know?

There are few laws of nature that beat this one, so make haste, my son. Start small, start gently, but start now. Do not wait to strike it big, for that route is very tortuous and slippery. I have seen enough men left waiting their whole lives for some dramatic game changer that never happens. I have come across enough men who lament on the 'misfortune' of expected or even 'guaranteed' big breaks not occurring.

This is one of the reasons I had to overcome my initial doubts and make the contents of these notes available to you as early as this. Don't sit around, my son.

7.5   What doesn't kill you

What doesn't kill you will make you stronger – really. Well, it is a saying in some parts of the world, used more to cheer up someone who has gone through a very bad experience, than anything else. It is meant to imply that the person would, in other words, have been made more resilient and tougher by the experience. It is meant to have more or less the same implication as the song 'The Harder They Come… the Harder They Fall" by Jimmy Cliff, but these are not the same.

What does not kill you is only ever going to stand a chance of toughening you up:

a) if you survive it. Exactly. What if the impact of the experience is enough to completely wipe you out? What would be there to learn if the damage was so much as to push you over that line of no return?

b) if some form of foundation has already been laid. Worse still is being taken through such a horrific experience in the absence of a necessary protective mechanism. It would be comparable to the difference between someone with some protective antibody load following a vaccination being attacked by the same dose of virus as a person who had absolutely no previous exposure. The impact of this 'small' difference could be deadly.

Another analogy is one that is quite well known within the medical world, some of the experiences unfortunately based on some nasty events. One of the worst was the devastating impact caused by the medication Thalidomide, a relatively harmless drug that even in overdose has not been associated with fatality or in fact major side effects.

Thalidomide was originally discovered in the 1950s and was initially mainly used for its calming effect in people who were very anxious or who could not sleep. These were, and remain, common problems, so the medication was widely used. The assumption of course was that it was really a harmless medication with some acceptable side effects like headache, dizziness, drowsiness and so on. It unfortunately took many years for the connection between the increasing number of babies born with either missing or severely deformed limbs and Thalidomide to emerge. The problem was that the severity of the side effects caused by this medication, as with all other medications, depended on what stage in one's life the medication was taken, and therein lies one of the best and clearest explanations of the butterfly effect. The younger the person involved in the incident, the more the likelihood that the impact of the

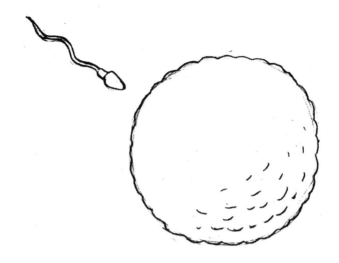

experience is going to be devastating. In the medical world, it is much easier and straightforward to explain using the phenomenon of fertilisation.

The process of fertilisation occurs when sperm (from a male) and a female egg join together. The genes from the man and the woman then combine to form a new life, the offspring. That point of contact of sperm and egg marks the beginning of the countdown. It is the most crucial and the most vulnerable, especially in terms of impact on the new being, the offspring. This period usually also marks the time when the offspring is most likely to die if confronted with a major setback or trauma. It could happen so quickly that the mother might not even be aware of having been pregnant!

In order to understand a few other things better, some further knowledge of what happens after fertilisation is necessary.

Remember we started off with two separate genes (from the man and the woman) coming together. What happens afterwards is that the fertilised egg then undergoes several divisions. If one major division of the fertilised egg happens (before the small numerous ones) then the pregnant woman ends up with identical twins. A critical point by this time is that the cells formed from the divisions are so unspecialised that any of them can become any part of the growing embryo. So, this marks the beginning of the next phase of development, and the next most critical phase, in terms of vulnerability. A difference to the point when the egg and the sperm come in contact is that from this point onwards, even though a major setback or trauma might not wipe out the cells, they could end up leaving a devastating impact.

Another way to look at it is from the perspective of a tree that has the possibility of growing into a massive tree, with up to seven branches. How the tree grows and develops depends of course on if (and which of) the branches are cut. More important, however, (which is where the butterfly effect comes in) is when the cut is made. If the cut is made early enough, you might not even need scissors, let alone a knife. Your thumbs could be enough. Think about cutting the same branch, or another branch off the same branch, years down the line. You would at such time need the help of an experienced professional.

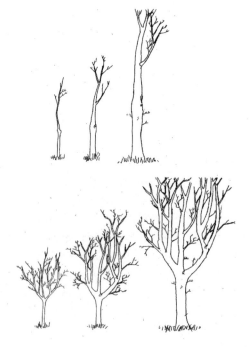

8

Live!

8.1 The worrier

There is a kind of person that people generally refer to as the 'worrier'. One of the things this person does is to constantly worry about most things, including the next stage or step. Problem is that there will ALWAYS be a next stage, and therefore something to worry about.

A worrier's wife is going to have a baby, and the worrier is mainly concerned about the health of the child, so much so that it gives him sleepless nights. What if the child is born with a handicap; what if there are complications and he loses his wife?

The wife gives birth without any problems but the worrier does not rejoice like every other person. No, he sits in a corner and is wondering about what would have happened if he had not brought his wife to the hospital in good time. How would he have coped with the situation? And then his mind wanders to the question, so how is he going to be sure that the child does not grow up to become like one of those kids in his neighbourhood; and what is the child going to become in life?

This is a man whose wife has just given birth to a child through a planned pregnancy.

From the above instance, it would be easy to realise that worrying about something does often not have any effect whatsoever on the issue being worried about, neither would it have any influence on what happens in the future. Often unknown to people who worry a lot, the aim of worrying is not necessarily to find a solution. One worries more out of fear of the unknown and about things one can hardly influence. For such people, worrying very quickly becomes a habit (a bad habit); a pastime. Like most habits, worrying becomes difficult to stop, and one becomes so used to it that one is even unable to imagine life without it. It becomes 'normal'. People around then refer to the person as a 'worrier', which unfortunately becomes a tag they have dangling round their necks for the rest of their lives.

If you think about it and try it, you would realise that one can, however, not be happy while worrying about something. A person who is intensively worrying about something would not be relaxed during the process. They would actually be tense. It is very difficult to see somebody genuinely smiling while deeply worrying about something – this is because smiling and worrying do not go hand in hand. When a person deeply worrying about something laughs it has a tendency to sound so false, so robotic.

It would then make sense to conclude that those who worry too much are tense most of the time and that they smile very little. One can take things further to say that such people are hardly happy, that they are often very moody and withdrawn. The above sounds very much like a recipe for body stiffness, aches and pain and the starting point for several forms of diseases.

The really sad thing is that the worrier could sit there and worry about something forever, but nothing changes. The issue or event causing them to worry does not change, nor does it go away.

Worrying about things does, funnily enough, also NOT make one more knowledgeable about the issue or event at hand. Worrying only makes an existing issue or problem appear much larger than it actually is. It exaggerates and blows things out of proportion.

Something that was originally so small that it was insignificant suddenly becomes a problem. Then after one would have thought about it from all sorts of angles, long enough, and worried enough about it, it then evolves into a really big problem.

8.2   Problems keep floating

While bearing in mind that a lot of people who worry a lot, unnecessarily, might not be able to help it as it sometimes also runs in families, it is worth noting, however, that a major problem is that people who worry a lot confuse worrying about something with researching or getting more information about an issue, which would be needed for decision making. This cannot be true, because they often do not even give themselves the space to find out more about the situation at hand. They do not get more knowledgeable about the topic that concerns them. Instead they make do with what they know, which is often not a lot and then try to work wonders with it. They also fail to realise that you can hardly make a decision during such 'worrying sessions'. What happens is that their thoughts just keep going round and round in circles, up and down, back and forth.

Decision making, on the other hand, means reaching a conclusion about what to do and forgetting all about the matter afterwards, so actually the opposite of worrying needlessly.

We all worry about things by nature, but some people seem to 'enjoy' it more. They could just sit there and drift into their dark world, where they could work bad magic on all sorts of various negative combinations and outcomes that various (often harmless) events could take. This is allowed to go on and on and on.

Worrying excessively has, however, no positive use. It is a complete waste of time, keeps people sad, and is the source of several illnesses.

Aim to stop worrying and live, because it is usually either of the two that would obtain – you are either out there living the life you want to, aiming for the sky, or you are spending a big chunk of your life worrying and thinking of what could be and what could have been. One of the things that additionally works against worrying is to take action. Any kind of positive action helps, even taking positive physical action could work wonders. Most people, who are in such energetic mode, would at such times struggle with just sitting down and doing nothing. The worrying usually builds up in momentum if they do. It is by far better to distract oneself by engaging in positive physical action. You will then find yourself gradually thinking of something else. But thinking you would, for we are made that way – we are always thinking about something. The good news is that we have the power to influence, or in fact decide on what to think about.

Put in the effort to break the habit. Guard your thought process like you would guard a box of immense treasure. Next time you feel yourself drifting into such thoughtful trances, jolt yourself out of it. Start by confronting your thoughts and by asking yourself, what am I thinking now? Reflect on what you're thinking, and ask yourself, does it make sense?

Ask yourself, would going ahead and thinking about what I am thinking about at the moment change anything, or is it a waste of time? It will become clear to you that you're not doing something progressive, assuming that to be the case at the time.

Ask yourself, do I have enough information to be able to make a decision? If you feel you have enough information, then make a decision about what to do and save your time. If you think you're not informed enough, then find means of getting the required information urgently so that your decision would be based on facts. Then, again, make that decision and devote your time to more productive things.

If you on the other hand find out that you're faced with one of such situations that you cannot influence, then even better. You at least then know it and it is also clear to you where you stand.

8.3   Don't bang your head

Have you ever tried to block the way for an ant with your finger?

If you haven't, then try it. Find an ant, place your finger in front of it to block its way and see what happens. If it goes round your finger, remove your finger and place it again in front of the ant. You will notice that the ant keeps going round your finger in its quest to find a way. The ant is unlikely to bite/sting you if you do not show any form of aggression.

It would in most cases not try to climb up your finger.

It does not stay there analysing your finger. It will most likely stop briefly, feel your finger and then move on. Once in a while, it will stop for breaks. As long as you do not irritate it, the same process will continue – almost for ever.

When the ant, however, gets tired or has had enough, do you know what it is likely to do? It is likely to walk away in the opposite direction, seemingly no longer interested.

There will be times when you will face obstacles, and I mean serious obstacles. I am talking of such challenges, of which the mere thought will leave you feeling terribly weak and numb. I am referring to the kind of situation where you would have absolutely no idea what to do, and the circumstances would be so overwhelming that making a decision would be close to impossible, mainly because you can hardly influence the sequence of events.

Do not lose it in such a situation. The underlying factor is that you cannot change the present situation of things. It could also be that an attempt to change things would require such drastic input from you that you could end up causing more harm than good – short or long term.

Those are the situations where you need to try hard to maintain your equilibrium. Save your energy in such circumstances, for you will soon be needing it. A worse thing still is to stand there thinking, "Why me?". Even more terrible, however, is to then start banging your head on the closed door. You will be wasting your time, your energy and pretty soon your blood. You could also cause serious damage to your head.

Learn from the ant, and know when to quickly and very briefly analyse a difficult situation, make a quick decision, follow your gut feeling and move on.

Go even further and just walk away if you're convinced the whole thing makes no sense.

Strange thing, of which I am sure, is that you will be both happy and grateful a few hours, days, weeks, months or years down the line that you did not just stand there banging your head on a closed door.

8.4   Don't confuse persistence with stubbornness

It is a great thing, very much worth working towards and aiming for, to be both consistent and persistent. Persistence is a virtue that will take you places you never imagined possible because very often the difference between the winner and the loser lies in the ability to be able to persevere, to go the extra distance when others would have given up. Persistence is a virtue that champions and geniuses alike all have. Nothing of significance gets accomplished without persistence.

Nothing. It is that powerful. As stated by Calvin Coolidge, nothing in the world can take the place of persistence. Talent will not; nothing is more common than unsuccessful men with talent. Genius will not; unrewarded genius is almost a proverb. Education will not; the world is full of educated derelicts. Persistence and determination alone are omnipotent.

I will also suggest looking up online the story of the donkey in the well.

It is, however, crucial to point out one very important mistake that I would want you to avoid. When you want something so badly, so desperately that you even go, in hindsight, to the extent of banging your head on a closed door, then catch yourself beforehand and reflect on what you're about to do. If doing all you have done and putting in all the effort you already have and making all the necessary sacrifices still does not open the door, then it might be time to consider stopping, and changing your approach. Standing in front of a closed door, a door clearly made of the best of woods, and consistently and intensively banging your head on it has absolutely NOTHING to do with persistence. Some people will prefer to call this stubbornness, as it sounds better than silliness. So, conserve your time and most importantly, your energy. You will need it for more necessary battles later. Learn from the ant. While keeping your eyes on the ultimate goal, adjust your plans and your strategy. This is real persistence. Don't bang your head, you need it for the challenges ahead. You will ultimately need to develop the capability of sensing when you need to keep digging, as a few more shovels could separate you from striking gold, or when to stop... just before banging your head.

8.5   Knowledge is *not* power

There is a large difference between wishfully doing something and actively doing something. They are in fact not related. There is a general belief that knowledge is power. This may, or may not be true, but instead depends on the circumstance and to what use acquired knowledge is put. You will be amazed by the number of people who have the knowledge to make an impact, but they do not. You will, in life, be surprised by lots of people who will want to be seen as gurus or experts, but who, on further enquiry, will be found to have failed in the exact same subject they claim specialist knowledge of. You will see wretched financial advisers and relationship counsellors who, themselves, have not experienced the wonderful impact of a functional relationship. You will come across a religious preacher practise outright hatred, which they also propagate. You will hear of priests whose hideous offences include that propagated against someone as vulnerable and innocent as a child. No, knowledge does not always equate to power because people often do not do the right thing, not because of ignorance or a lack of knowledge, but because of factors more entrenched, deeper and sinister than that. People could, therefore, despite being equipped with the necessary information, not make that required move. They would still not take the action needed.

There are similarly lots of people in situations they thoroughly hate; people who face circumstances that keep them sad or in fear. All that would be required would be for them to rise to the occasion – to make the necessary decision and stick to it and to follow things up with some action. The sad bit is that they, as already mentioned, could be aware of this, they might even know exactly what to do, but somehow, they don't. Knowledge in their case is certainly not power; it is actually nothing. It is wasted knowledge and has neither meaning nor relevance, for what use is knowledge if it exists but is not put to any use?

8.6   Switch off the TV

Few things are as time-consuming, stupidity-perpetuating and detrimental to yourself and the general world view as uncontrolled TV watching.

Part of the problem is with the mass media needing to grab our attention and the fact that they thrive on sensationalism. So, the more horrible and grotesque the incident, the more exciting they find it. If it's not exciting enough, they spice it up a bit if needs be. It often looks as if a major aim of the mass media is to keep reminding us of what is not working in society. It is a narrow and perverted view of the world that could not only contaminate our world view, but also quite negatively affect our creative potential.

A little bit of distraction, once in a while, is a necessity, but one which uncontrolled and prolonged TV watching is unlikely to serve. In this day and age, this applies maybe even more to use of/visits to certain websites that compete for your attention for images and videos. We live in the Information Age, but the constant question should be, what information are you potentially clogging up your brain with?

8.7   What if you die tonight?

There is something people who have survived a terminal illness, or other life-threatening situations, have always talked about. They all describe a life similar to being born again, when they noticed that, contrary to medical opinion (in the case of a terminal illness), they are coping fine and then go ahead to live better and longer than predicted. They all comment on leading a much more conscious life. They generally describe the kind of life they live after the pronouncement that they would soon die as being much higher in intensity.

They become grateful for every new day, and appreciate much more the things they would ordinarily have overlooked. After they have come to terms and accepted the fact that they could die at any time, the fear associated with dying then becomes significantly reduced. Every day is a gift that they are thankful for and the days are treated as such – something special.

People who believe that they do not have long to live think less complicatedly and live with a lot of passion. They do not take too many wrongdoings by others to heart – it is not important, they think; there are more important things in life. This makes them additionally much more forgiving and open to reconciliation. They do not have room for grudges.

Just think about it, would it not be a good thing to go through life then as if the end was near and we didn't have long to live?

Would it not add a lot of spice to life? If just thinking that we do not have long to live can have such dramatic effect on our outlook to life, why not aim to think we have but a short time to live all the time? We can at any point in time think whatever we want to, so that there is certainly nothing that would stop us from occupying our mind with such thoughts.

So, try it and see. Imagine that you have but a short time to live – what would your thought process be; how would you feel? Think about it.

If you actually come to think about it, the truth is that we actually do not know how long we will live. The only sure and clear thing is that we will all die – when, where and how, nobody knows. So, it is effectively the truth that we might not have long to live, that we might not make tomorrow.

Next thing that is often good to reflect on is – if one were to die this very minute, would one die a happy and content person? Bear in mind that that is the way people with terminal illnesses are forced to think. This is the kind of thought they're occupied with most of the time. From the reflections above, I am sure that it's obvious that even people who seem healthy, might actually not have long to live. We therefore have to ask ourselves the same question that somebody who does formally not have long to live would have to constantly ask him or herself – if we were to now drop dead, would we have died a happy and fulfilled person?

Do all you can to be in this state of mind as often as possible – it will certainly lighten up your life and help you live life to the fullest.

8.8   Live with passion

Live, my son, live.

Live like your life depends on it.

Live without fear, for the world belongs to those who are able to erase the word fear from their vocabulary.

Live with gratitude in your heart. Appreciate the good things that have happened in your life. Do this every day, every hour. It makes it easier to see things, and life, positively. It makes it easier to have good thoughts in your mind most of the time. You become more optimistic and tend to see the brighter side of circumstances.

There is a belief that you are what you think, or put differently, what you think, you become. If you are depressed, and think and believe that you are depressed, then your depression becomes worse and this affects the sort of thoughts that go through your mind and your outlook generally.

If you think you are good enough to be one of the best pupils in your class, or even your school, you will certainly get to that status, I guarantee you. Your mind, you and all the forces surrounding you will do everything to make sure you attain the level you yearn for. Your hopes and desires become a challenge for your unconscious self.

There are many theories about what happens when we die. Until such speculations can be substantiated with proof and evidence that can be verified scientifically, they remain just that – speculations.

So what matters most is what you do with the life you have been given while you are alive, and to an extent the type of legacy you want to leave when you die. You are young, I know, but nothing stops you from thinking that far.

Make the most of life. See the world. Get exposed to different ideas. This way you learn to have broader views; to be more open-minded. It is then easier to see the whole picture; to be more imaginative.

Dare to reach for the sky. Don't be afraid. Do not think about falling. Once you as much as ponder over falling, it is all over. You become exposed to the torture of analysing how you're going to fall. What kind of sound will you make? Where will you land? Will you fall on your back; on your head, and break your neck, or will you land on your knees? What will the people around do? Will there be anybody around when you fall? Will they help you? Will they laugh at you and wonder why you thought you could go for the sky in the first place? Will your friends desert you?

Once you bring your mind into this kind of state, it will hardly be able to stop. You are afterwards left exhausted and ultimately happy to be alive. Who wants to get to the sky? you would wonder. And before you know it, you're on your way, falling, exactly as you had expected you would.

But then what is wrong in falling? It is another natural process – if you are not aligned in proportion to your centre of gravity, you fall. The problem is not with falling itself. As a child while learning to stand and then to walk I lost count of how many times you fell. Did I stop you from learning to walk? Of course not. You certainly would not have allowed me to stop you from walking anyway.

So why was it OK and acceptable to fall as a child, but then something to be terrified of as an adult? The truth is that each time you fall you learn something, thus becoming better. You also become more confident. So, falling is something good. The ultimate joy, however, lies in getting up after each fall, no matter how bad the fall was and the injuries sustained.

Aiming for the best is not the easiest thing to do, but that alone is worth it. If you aim for the sky and miss, do you know what will happen? The clouds will catch and embrace you. They will wrap their arms around you and wipe your eyes. Your position is by no means comparable to that of the person who was content with crawling. It is said that the old woman who walks with a stick will neither run nor dance till she has thrown away the stick.

There's joy in living life to the maximum. It is fulfilling. As human beings, we are endowed with amazing capabilities. Make use of even a fraction of this in order to be of use to yourself and to the human race.

I dare not forget to remind you to be sure to enjoy the flight to the sky. The journey may last forever; you may only get there towards the end of your time. You may even get there and then realise that you interpreted the compass wrongly and therefore travelled in the wrong direction; that you therefore landed on the moon instead of the Mars you wanted to get to. This could be frustrating, and life is too short. So, aim for the sky, but make sure you're having fun and enjoying the journey. Actually, the most important thing may not be the point you want to get to. It could well be the journey itself, especially as you could be spending quite a lot of time on the journey. Life at the top is sometimes also short-lived. It is not unusual for people to get there and then to wonder – is this all there is to it; was this the reason I went through all the trouble? Problem is that you wouldn't know what you would feel until you get there, so don't let what you could think when you get to the top deter you. Worse are people who spend their whole life dreaming and wishing. It is worse because they will never know. Theirs is a life that would be spent wondering what it would have been like, what would have been. Be nice, be humble and understanding, but have the courage to be impatient if you have to.

Have the courage to go for it – whatever IT is. Do not worry about falling, there's nothing wrong with that. Be concerned if you have the feeling that you could have problems motivating yourself to get up after you fall. But don't stop there – work on it.

Go a little further, grow wings, and learn to fly.

About the Author

DR OKECHUKWU MICHAEL MWIM studied medicine in Vienna. His journey from Africa to Austria was not the most conventional and this, with his time in Austria, required enormous amounts of grit. He emigrated to London after completing his studies, and has since practised medicine. He also engages in various entrepreneurial activities.

Author's Note

My Rich Prince is based on a compilation of essential, and sometimes personal, notes originally put together, over several years, by Michael for his young child. It is perceived a must read for every young person and has at its core general advice and messages about fulfilment in life, responsibility and achieving one's potential.